Tender LEAVES of HOPE

I encourage every Latter-day Saint to read this book. If you are LGBTQ or want to better support LGBTQ Latter-day Saints, Meghan's book will help you. Meghan does a wonderful and courageous job of sharing her story as a gay Latter-day Saint and also bringing to light many other stories of LGBTQ Latter-day Saint women. I'm grateful to Meghan and all who shared their stories and their efforts to help us better create Zion.

—Richard Ostler, author of *Listen, Learn, and Love*
and host of *Questions from the Closet* podcast

While she is a powerful and skilled educator, the real beauty of Meghan's work is her desire to step to the sideline and elevate the stories of other queer women. She recognizes that she is not the only one who has been called to share her story and that many thousands of others will feel and have felt that call as well. Meghan's courage and authenticity will help cultivate "tender leaves of hope" in those who read her story. Church leaders will see how they can minister more effectively, families will better understand their LGBTQ loved ones, and women like Meghan will build Zion as they share their hearts and minds with their communities.

—Ben Schilaty, author of *A Walk in My Shoes:
Questions I'm Often Asked as a Gay Latter-day Saint*
and co-host of *Questions from the Closet* podcast

Tender LEAVES of HOPE

Finding Belonging as LGBTQ Latter-day Saint Women

MEGHAN DECKER

CFI

AN IMPRINT OF CEDAR FORT, INC. • SPRINGVILLE, UTAH

ISBN 13: 978-1-4621-4328-3

Published by CFI, an imprint of Cedar Fort, Inc.
2373 W. 700 S., Springville, UT 84663
Distributed by Cedar Fort, Inc., www.cedarfort.com

Library of Congress Control Number: 2022930827

Cover design by Shawnda T. Craig
Cover design © 2022 Cedar Fort, Inc.
Edited and typeset by Spencer Skeen

Printed in the United States of America

10 9 8 7 6 5 4 3 2 1

Printed on acid-free paper

I am indebted to the remarkable women who bravely shared their stories with me. To them, and all who walk the same road with us, I dedicate this work.

Ad Dei gloriam

Prayer of St. Francis

Lord, make me a channel of thy peace,
That where there is hatred, I may bring love,
That where there is wrong, I may bring the spirit of forgiveness,
That where there is discord, I may bring harmony,
That where there is error, I may bring truth,
That where there is doubt, I may bring faith,
That where there is despair, I may bring hope,
That where there are shadows, I may bring light,
That where there is sadness, I may bring joy.
Lord, grant that I may seek rather to comfort than to be comforted,
To understand, than to be understood,
To love, than to be loved.
For it is by self-forgetting that one finds.
It is by forgiving that one is forgiven.
It is by dying that one is raised to eternal life.
Amen.

Contents

Foreword

by Ben Schilaty

In early 2020 I received a Facebook message request from Meghan Decker. She had some questions for an article she was writing, and we exchanged a few messages. I thought that was the end of the conversation. Then in December 2020, after months of silence, I received a message from her that said, in part, "I'd love to talk on the phone—sorry, you don't know me, and that feels like a big ask, but I'm asking anyway." We talked that evening. Even though we were basically strangers, she came out to me on the phone that night. After that we were friends for life.

I immediately sensed that Meghan would have a big impact in the LGBTQ Latter-day Saint world. In a space that is dominated by men, I knew that Meghan's voice was precisely what many were craving. I told her that she needed to write a book so that women like her could read a story similar to their own. From time to time, I would get a message from a gay woman married to a man, asking if I knew of anyone like them that they could talk to. I asked Meghan if she would be willing to talk to these women, and she told me she would be delighted to talk to all of them. She happily spoke with every one of them I sent to her.

In June 2021, Meghan sat in the makeshift recording studio in my basement and recorded an episode for the *Questions from the Closet* podcast titled "Is it ever too late to come out?" Meghan had come out publicly only weeks before, so sharing her story on the podcast was a bold, courageous thing to do. She did not have to do this. She could have easily spent her golden years doting on her grandkids, but instead she chose the harder path of public vulnerability. Her story instantly resonated with many, and I received multiple emails from closeted women in similar situations.

Meghan, like many others, has "come to the kingdom for such a time as this" (Esther 4:14). As a grandmother, former Relief Society president and early morning Seminary teacher, and wife intent on creating a successful and happy marriage, she lives a life that feels familiar and comfortable to Latter-day Saints who have been hesitant to learn about LGBTQ Latter-day Saint experiences. While she is a powerful and skilled educator, the real beauty of Meghan's work is her desire to step to the sideline and elevate the stories of other queer women. She recognizes that she is not the only one who has been called to share her story and that many thousands of others will feel and have felt that call as well. Meghan's courage and authenticity will help cultivate "tender leaves of hope" in those who read her story. Church leaders will see how they can minister more effectively, families will better understand their LGBTQ loved ones, and women like Meghan will build Zion as they share their hearts and minds with their communities. This book is a continuation of the work that has been done for decades by LGBTQ Latter-day Saints, and it will inspire many to join that labor.

Meghan's story is far from over, and this book represents only a chapter of her life. I'm so pumped to see how our Heavenly Parents will call on her and many others in the coming years to build the kingdom.

Introduction

I feel hope in the early spring, when tiny leaf buds appear as proof that the Michigan winter is going to release its hold. I love those first bright green leaves. They are tender and young and fresh, and the trees appear to be enveloped in a pale green mist. Those young leaves hold the promise of summer's maturity, when I will lie in my hammock and look up at the dappled light coming through maple, oak, sassafras, and hickory leaves that have grown bigger than my hand.

Hope begins that way, as a tender spring leaf with the promise of summer's lush shade and beauty. Hope in Christ sustains me every day, and when I nourish it, I have shelter and peace. Hope gives life and a promise of eventual joy.

When I started writing this book, interviews with other women were almost an afterthought. I realized that my experience as a gay Latter-day Saint woman is different from many other LGBTQ women in the Church, and I thought it would be helpful to speak to a few others. I reached out through a Facebook group and asked if anyone would be willing to talk to me.

Those "few others" eventually became over three dozen women, and hearing their stories has been my favorite part of writing this book. We share an attraction to women and experience in the Church, but the way those commonalities impact our lives is different for all of us. I am indebted to their vulnerability and trust, and I am in awe of their beautiful, strong, loving, and hopeful hearts. They are precious to God.

The stories I share here, including my own, represent a moment in time. Our lives will continue to develop, and we will increase in understanding as we continue to learn through our own experiences. There may be unanticipated turns in the road, but this is where we are today.

I think of two groups as I write: the first are people who want to be supportive to friends, family, and Church members who experience same-sex attraction or gender dysphoria, and/or who identify as LGBTQ. These readers have positive intent, but they fear making painful mistakes. They want to learn, and I hope this book helps to increase their empathy and understanding.

The second group, dear to my heart, are women who also experience attraction to women and may feel isolated, ashamed, and hopeless. Knowing they are not alone in the Church can create a profound paradigm shift. As I have been more open about my own situation, I have been surprised by the women who quietly sought me out—many who have been hiding these feelings, assuming they were broken and unacceptable to God. Yet they continue to serve Him with all their hearts while suffering in seclusion. Active Latter-day Saints who experience same-sex attraction are rarely visible. I have much to say to these good sisters, but here is the most important truth: God loves you, just as you are. He knows you, and He loves you, every bit of you. "For we are so preciously loved by God that we cannot even comprehend it. . . . all shall be well, and all shall be well, and all manner of thing shall be well."[1]

Thank you for caring, for picking up this book, for opening your heart to me and my friends, and for seeking out your people. I hope that as you read, you will feel the Spirit testify to you of God's love for his LGBTQ children and for you.

Notes for Introduction

1   Julian of Norwich, Showings: Julian of Norwich (Mahwah, NJ: Paulist Press, 1978).

TIMELINE OF MY LIFE IN REFERENCE TO SAME-SEX ATTRACTION

ABOUT 1975—I go into hiding and denial for decades

1979-2018—Periodic episodes of depression triggered by shame, some with suicidal ideation

FALL 2013—I come out to myself

CHRISTMAS EVE 2013—I open up to David, my husband

EARLY JANUARY 2014—I leave for Utah to help a daughter with a health crisis. I read *Sexual Fluidity* and reach out to Laurie Campbell, author of *Born That Way?*, for help to understand myself, my sexual orientation, and what my future can or should be.

SPRING 2014—Despite the help, I find myself feeling exhausted, confused, and scared. I put any discussion of my sexual orientation back on the shelf for the next four years. I continue to think about what I've learned and what it means for me.

EARLY 2018—I talk to my friend about my depression and wanting to find greater emotional stability. I learn more about shame, and I start talking to David again about same-sex attraction. I eventually talk to a few more friends, finding the antidote to shame in speaking my truth and being met with empathy and compassion.

SUMMER 2018—Romantic feelings come up in a friendship; I work with a therapist and experience an intensive learning period. I talk to my daughters about my SSA for the first time.

SPRING 2021—I open up to my mom and brother, David's mother and siblings, then broadly to many friends. I start speaking and writing openly about my life as a gay Latter-day Saint.

Chapter One

GROW AS WE GO

I am a woman who is attracted to women. I am also happily married to an amazing man. We have children and grandchildren together, and we are "all in" concerning our covenants and church service. People in our stake might be surprised to know we have not lived a life of spiritual ease.

I've served as Relief Society president, temple ordinance worker, seminary teacher, Primary president, institute teacher, and in various stake callings and presidencies. I support my husband, David, in his demanding leadership callings. We have five daughters and fifteen grandchildren. We've done our best to teach them the gospel of Jesus Christ. I've studied, prayed, and fasted. I have deep faith in the Atonement of Jesus Christ. I trust in His mercy and love.

I am still attracted to women.

Ten years ago, I was hiding that truth from everyone, including myself. My denial was so strong that I could answer questions in seminary about same-sex attraction without even a thought for my own complicated feelings. I created firewalls between the life I wanted to live and my continuing magnetic pull toward women, and I didn't allow conscious thought past those firewalls. I didn't see how my deep faith and my attraction to women could coexist. So I did everything I could to ignore and bury my same-sex attraction. I was doing the best I knew how, but this coping strategy took a terrible toll on my mental health and my relationships with my family and with God.

I have now opened up about my feelings for women, the feelings I desperately hid for most of my life. It is a profound seismic shift, one I would never have imagined. What could create such a change? Only love: the confidence and peace that comes from feeling and believing the love of my Heavenly Parents and my Savior; the love and acceptance I feel for myself; the love and trust I feel from my family and my friends; and the love and compassion I feel for those I don't yet know who feel alone and scared.

Perhaps you are in the midst of this tortuous and terrifying and immensely rewarding journey. I don't want you to have to do it alone. I wish I could sit next to you and share my story. I'll do that in the pages to come—I'll share with you the events that brought me to this place of love, peace, empathy, and delicate balance. My life isn't a road map for anyone else, but perhaps you will find something useful for your situation. I'll discuss the concepts that enlightened my understanding, as well as my deepening appreciation of the nature of God, His plan for my growth, and the wondrous ways I see Him working in my life. I will also share the insights of more than forty women, all Latter-day Saint and LGBTQ[1], who are motivated by love to share what they have experienced and learned.

I'm ready to come out of hiding because I want to share what I've learned. I am mostly free from the shame that crushed me for years. I know my attraction for women will not disappear as a reward for good behavior, and I don't want it to. I don't want to lose the gifts that accompany my orientation toward women. I also know that, while I can't decide to change my sexual orientation, I *can* decide how I respond to the circumstances of my life. Those responses are not the answers on my final exam. I'm nowhere near the end of the semester. I'm still actively learning, taking pop quizzes, correcting what I misunderstood, and trying an answer and finding it's not the one I really want. I am moving toward greater internal harmony and external unity with my family, faith community, and God.

I recognize I had placed a box of imposed expectations around God. My assumptions limited my full experience of His love, patience, creativity, and desire for me to learn. I often find myself repeating to myself, "God said, 'Surprise!'" I've learned He values growth over a perfect test score, and that is both frightening and humbling. It changes my perspective of His Plan of Happiness, and it reminds me I am a child growing into a godly inheritance, not a servant simply meeting obligations and fulfilling duties. I am learning from my experience to understand and emulate the true nature of God. I have more questions and less certainty, and it surprises me to realize this is forward movement on the covenant path.

I used to be scared of my attraction to women being discovered, of losing my family and possibly my faith, and of giving up control of my life and being at the mercy of forces I didn't choose. I was fragmented, fractured into pieces: my faith, my family, my shame over attractions I didn't understand—all colliding with each other in such fearful ways that I did all I could to compartmentalize them.

Today, I know that I am an agent who acts, not a passive player who is "acted upon" (2 Nephi 2:14). Most importantly, I'm not alone in this. I know that God is deeply involved in the lives of His LGBTQ children, wherever they are on their journey through mortality. For many of them, personal revelation is the norm, not the exception. They find that God is generous with His guidance and comfort. I'm no longer fearful of watching my family or my faith slip away. I can choose my own path forward. I also know, from lived experience revealing the deepest desires of my heart, what I will choose.

I feel a profound optimism for LGBTQ members of the church and those within their sphere of influence. When I talk to the many gay women who have come out of hiding to tell their story, I see how their openness is affecting their family, friends, and ward family who can grow into a suspension of judgment and an increase of Christlike love. As they open up to others, LGBTQ Latter-day Saints may experience healing, greater trust in many relationships, a release of shame, and improved mental health. Their openness creates opportunities for healing and growth among everyone involved. Could this be one way the Lord is preparing His people for His return—a way to help us increase in the kind of love that is less conditioned on social conformity or rigid interpretations and more focused on the pure love of Christ? Elder D. Todd Christofferson taught:

> First, and crucial for the Lord's return, is the presence on the earth of a people prepared to receive Him at His coming. . . . The Prophet

Joseph Smith stated, "We ought to have the building up of Zion as our greatest object." We build up Zion in our homes, wards, branches, and stakes through unity, godliness, and charity.[2]

One of my daughters is queer, and I belong to a Facebook group for parents of Latter-day Saint LGBTQ children. I consistently see parents express their gratitude for a deeper and more unconditional love for their child. That no-strings-attached love often develops as they grapple with their own feelings about their child's orientation or gender identity. Perhaps we are becoming a more righteous people because we are becoming more loving, patient, and merciful—more like our Heavenly Parents. As one mother of two LGBTQ children stated, *"We're building love like no generation has ever seen before."*

Though there may be some parallels among us, my journey is not the roadmap for all LDS women attracted to women. I would be horrified if someone gives this book to you and says "See, you can do what she did." Nothing about being a Latter-day Saint and LGBTQ is off the rack—everything about our lives is custom-made, tailored for us according to our past, our personality, our circumstances, our opportunities, and, most importantly, our desires. God doesn't force us into becoming something different from our truest selves. He will lovingly and tenderly stay with us as we drop our damaging and false expectations of what we "should" be to become free to discern the true desires of our hearts. I believe God will help us to know ourselves as He knows us.

TRUTHS FOR MY LIFE

Here are some truths that I have discovered along the way, and which you may find helpful. As they say in Twelve Step meetings, take what you need and leave the rest:

- I realize I am not alone.
- I reject the false belief that I am too broken to be acceptable to God.
- I also reject the insinuation that my marriage is doomed to unhappiness and failure.
- I tear down the shame that was the wallpaper of my life.

- I discern, through my lived experience and agency, what matters most to me.
- I continue to integrate my faith with my sexual orientation, moving from dissonance to harmony.
- I realize the power of agency to seek out God's customized tutoring for my specific circumstances.
- I decide how I will respond to the choices before me.
- I accept the responsibility to seek revelation and "Hear Him," rather than outsourcing inspiration and looking to others to tell me what to do.
- I recognize the importance of actually "Hearing Him," rather than imposing my limited expectations of what I *think* He would say.
- I understand that "sexual orientation" refers to much more than sexual attraction—it is a composite of emotional, intellectual, spiritual, aesthetic, and a hard-to-pin-down magnetic pull to another gender and/or person.
- I discover that there are gifts of the Spirit that accompany my multi-dimensional attraction to women.
- I feel love and acceptance at church, which makes it a safe space for me to worship, grow, serve, and be served. The members who go out of their way to make a place for me are bearing living witness of their commitment to a covenant relationship with God and His children.
- I am grateful to see the arm of the Lord revealed as He works in the lives of His children to increase their love for one another.

I discovered a musical equivalent to my experience in Ben Platt's song "Grow As We Go." I hear God encouraging me to stay close to Him, to change next to Him rather than turning away. He makes space for my highs and lows, and He lets me know that I can take the time I need. Growth is a process, sometimes slow and convoluted, and I don't need to race to get to where *I expect* He wants me to be. I can stay near Him as we find my way forward together.

I also see how my husband David and I are able to grow individually, yet not in isolation. We are different, and better, than when we started down this difficult road. David offers me grace and respects my agency—he is willing to walk this unusual road with me. We move ahead side by side, and we don't retreat to our separate corners to figure things out. Neither of us have decided we can't do this anymore. Staying next to one another enables us to learn and give support in the process. I don't know how many people can manage this, but I'm grateful we have come to this place. It took time, patience, a whole lot of work, and miracles.

I hope that, as I share my life with you and insights from others, you will recognize that you are not alone. We are part of a group that is perhaps unenviable but also holy, sanctified by our suffering and faith. And we are known to God.

My expectations of how quickly the Spirit would flee kept me in a place of shame and dread for much of my life. I thought my feelings meant I was broken, tainted, and damaged beyond repair. I believed God was waiting for me to misstep and then would pounce in condemnation. The greatest gift I've received from my attraction to women is an enlightened appreciation of God's patience, tenderness, and mercy as He gently and persistently invites me to expand my understanding, abandon my flawed expectations, and trust Him.

Binary, either/or thinking doesn't fit with the reality of my life or my understanding of God's plan for His children. His plan is big enough to allow space for also/and. I experience romantic feelings for women, AND I am a faithful member of the church. I love my husband deeply, AND I feel attracted to women. God wants me to choose Him though my covenants, AND He will sit with me in my yearning for what is outside the bounds He has set. I can yearn to kiss a woman, AND have His Spirit with me. I no longer feel broken. I don't feel my orientation toward women is a flaw of mortality. I don't feel wrong or deserving of rejection. I don't want God to take this from me, and I don't believe He would.

I also don't want to lose my deep appreciation and love for women, the closeness to my Savior that I've experienced as I have come to Him in my tears and despair, the empathy and compassion I've developed, or the forged and tempered determination to honor my covenants and be faithful to my husband. There is a beautiful part of this experience that is filled with light and peace and joy. For years, my shame kept me from seeing things as they really are and appreciating these gifts.

I learned, from my lived experience, that the constant in my life is God. Through trial and error, through sin and obedience, through my own experience of good, evil, depression, anxiety, desire, suicidal ideation, attractions, anger, joy, pain, happiness—I know that I *always* come back to Him. He is my center, my comfort, my place. Whatever brings me to Him is good. My covenants create a bond with Christ that I treasure.

If you are reading right now because you have a loved one who is LGBTQ, thank you for your compassion and desire to understand their experience. If you identify as LGBTQ, or wonder if you might, I wish we could sit together. I would ask you to tell me your story, listen, and let you be messy without judgment.

You have a Savior who knows you better than you know yourself, who suffers beside you and who will carry your burdens and enlighten your understanding. He will sit with you in your pain and understand the conflicting, clashing passions inside of you. He has compassion for you, and He will help you if you'll let Him. You are not alone.

Notes for Chapter One

1   If you are new to this topic, you may wonder what the letters in LGBTQ mean. They represent *Lesbian* for women attracted to women; *Gay*, which originally meant a man attracted to men but now is often used as a casual term for anyone attracted to their own gender; *Bisexual* for people who are consistently attracted to both their own and the opposite gender; *Transgender*, which refers not to sexual orientation but to gender identity and represents people who experience gender dysphoria (feeling they are in the wrong body or were assigned the wrong gender at birth); and *Queer*, a former slur that has been rehabilitated to mean outside of the box of straight and cisgender ("cisgender" or "cis" means the person identifies with the gender assigned at birth). There are many other terms and descriptions that people use for themselves, and as you'll see later, often people move from one to another to find the right fit. They may also reject any category at all for the complicated reality of their lives.

2   D. Todd Christofferson, "Preparing for the Lord's Return," *Ensign*, May 2019.

Chapter Two

I AM NOT ALONE

The tension between my covenant life (which I love) and my attraction to women (I love them, too) has played emotional havoc in my life. Eventually I fell to my knees before the Savior and brought all my shame and pain to Him. He led me to a place of tension between two realities that leaves me space in the middle to know God and find peace.

I am one of many Latter-day Saint women who experience same-sex attraction and remain committed to activity in the church and to my family. I know my life and choices are not representative of all lesbian, gay, bisexual, or queer women or transgender men and women. There are a surprising number of us who live within these two realities, covenant women and LGBTQ. We are not often visible. For this part of our lives, our voices are quiet, even mute.

In an effort to amplify women's voices and experiences beyond my own, I conducted interviews with over forty women who live at the intersection of being both a Latter-day Saint and an LGBTQ individual. I wanted to understand each of their unique journeys through this space. I draw on those discussions for this book, but I honor their privacy by using pseudonyms instead of their names. They are not representative of all LGBTQ women who come from a Latter-day Saint background; most of the women I talked to want to maintain some sort of relationship with the church. Some of them bear powerful testimony of the Book of Mormon even as they affirm their decision to date women. Others are committed to keeping their covenants and the standards of the church, while they grapple every day with a deep yearning to partner with a woman. These women have shared some of the most painful and sacred moments of their lives. I am deeply moved by their suffering and strength and faith.

What do feelings of same-sex attraction mean for women who are committed to keeping their gospel covenants? They may strive with all their hearts to do everything they believe God, their families, and their community expect of them; however, these confusing feelings of desire and loss run deep.

When I was in this agony of conflicting desires, I felt lonely and hopeless. I was detached from friends and family because my inner life was so incongruent with how people viewed me.

For years the dissonance and the accompanying shame caused profound damage. I'm not alone. Many Latter-day Saint women experience same-sex attraction, and while their lives differ in the details, here are a few examples that may sound familiar:

- A married Latter-day Saint woman became physically involved with her best friend for a short time. While she repented with the Lord and her bishop, decades later she continues to feel a deep brokenness and shame.
- A sister daydreams of sexual involvement with a friend who is kind and thoughtful and who cares deeply about her, in contrast to her experience in an emotionally-starved marriage. She would not identify as bisexual or gay, but she finds herself unexpectedly feeling romantic attractions to her friend.
- A returned missionary young adult woman fell in love with her best friend in high school, a roommate in college, and a companion on her mission. Each time she experienced profound depressive episodes with suicidal thoughts. She tried to make up for her perceived brokenness with scrupulous obedience to gospel principles and mission rules. Eventually she admitted to herself and to God that she is gay, and she is seeking her way forward in the church while also hoping for marriage and family with a woman.
- A woman who identifies as lesbian remains married to a man,

committed to her family and her covenants but feeling the grief of never having the kind of relationship that feels most natural to her.

- A divorced single mother has a testimony of the gospel and feels the way forward for her is through a relationship with her girlfriend. She wants to continue attending church with her children and worship in whatever way is permitted by her local leaders.

- A mother has a daughter who has come out as gay. The mother is trying to understand what her daughter is experiencing and is unsure of how the family should respond, how they can show their love, and even whether the girl should be allowed to have LGBTQ friends over. This mom has many questions. She wants to act in the best possible way but hears conflicting voices telling her what that response should be.

- An active, married Latter-day Saint woman is engaged in an emotional and physical affair with her friend from church. Their relationship creates a fragmentation of their visible and hidden lives as well as their covenant-keeping and covenant-breaking actions.

- A woman was in a deeply satisfying same-sex relationship until she felt God call her out of that relationship and back to church. She later married a man and had a family, all the while navigating her continued attraction to women. She has built a satisfying emotional and spiritual relationship with her husband.

- A single woman is only physically attracted to women but hears the Lord telling her, "Your path is to keep the commandments." She feels the Lord's presence and support most strongly when she is praying to Him about her attraction to women.

None of these stories is finished, wrapped up in a lovely package with a bow on top. Every life is a dynamic work in progress. Most of these women share a feeling of isolation and moving outside a script that appears to work for everyone else, but there is also a recurrent theme of feeling God working in their lives and giving them specific and compassionate guidance.

HOW DO YOU IDENTIFY?

When I open up and share my story, one of the questions I am often asked is how I identify; people seem to feel more comfortable if they know my category. Some would say "bisexual" is most descriptive of my life because I am married to a man, but that feels like I'm wearing a pair of shoes that don't quite fit. I am not attracted to men and women; I am attracted to David and women, a manifestation of sexual fluidity (which I'll discuss in greater depth later). When I talk to people about this aspect of my life, I typically say I am gay. "Gay" technically refers to men attracted to men, but it has become a blanket term that women use as well, especially if they dislike "lesbian." The meaning of "gay" has expanded from identifying someone in a same-sex relationship to include anyone who is primarily oriented toward their own gender, regardless of behavior. "Queer" is most inclusive, but because it used to be an insult, it can be confusing or off-putting to friends who are just starting to learn about the LGBTQ community.

In my interviews with LGBTQ women, "How do you identify?" is one of the first questions I ask. I rarely get a quick or definitive answer. Some women are comfortable with "lesbian," but others have a dislike for the term. If they are also in a mixed-orientation marriage, meaning they are attracted to women but married to a man, they may feel they can't use "lesbian." But "bisexual" doesn't capture the reality of their lives because they are not consistently attracted to men as they are to women.

In the Church we often use the term "same-sex attraction" (SSA) as a descriptor, but many members find that saying "I experience same-sex attraction" diminishes the multi-dimensional quality of their orientation toward women. They intensely dislike the phrases "struggles with," "suffers from," or even "has," as if they are afflicted with a disease.

These are some of the responses I received when I asked women*
how they identify:

- Several women said they first used the term SSA, then bisexual,
  then gay, as they became more comfortable with themselves
  and their feelings.
- McKell used to say "experiences SSA," and now says "gay and
  married to a man."
- Joy prefers fluid; others would say she is bisexual.
- Daniela describes herself as queer. She explains she dislikes
  saying "I have SSA" as if it were a cold.
- River surprised me with "Popeye—I am who I am."
- Phoebe is bisexual and finds it frustrating that other people
  see her as either not gay enough or too gay.
- "I identify as Cindy. We are each unique, and my story isn't
  like anyone else's."
- Beth used to say lesbian. "When I started coming back to
  church, I switched to SSA; now I just say I am me. Queer has
  become more attractive. The longer I'm back on the gospel
  path, the less I need a term."
- Several women described themselves as attracted to women—
  and one particular man.

I, like many others, most closely identify with the last. I wish
we had a word that describes that complicated reality of being oriented toward women and one man. I find "fluid" to be most fitting,
based on Dr. Lisa Diamond's research. She says that "Sexual fluidity,
quite simply, means situation-dependent flexibility in women's sexual
responsiveness. This flexibility makes it possible for some women to
experience desires for either men or women under certain circumstances, regardless of their overall sexual orientation. . . . women of all
orientations may experience variation in their erotic and affectional
feelings as they encounter different situations, relationships, and life

---

* All names have been changed, though some of the women I interviewed would
have preferred to use their own name. They have fought a battle to come to a
place of openness and honesty about who they are, and they didn't want to surrender that authenticity. I appreciate their graciousness in allowing me to have
my way and shield their identities.

stages."[1] This factor of female sexuality explains how a lesbian can find herself in love with a man, or a heterosexual woman might be surprised by feelings of romantic and sexual attraction for her friend.

Fluidity can account for surprising attractions not aligned with one's fundamental sexual orientation, but it can't be manipulated at will. Dr. Diamond notes that "it is critically important to differentiate between the forms of change . . . which can be described as 'unintentional' change, and changes which result from individuals' effortful attempts to eliminate their same-sex attractions. . . . There is currently no evidence that therapeutic attempts to extinguish same-sex attractions are effective, and in fact those attempts have been found to cause psychological harm."[2] The potential for fluidity in women's attractions is not an invitation to "pray the gay away" or a justification for conversion therapy, which has been condemned by the Church and mental health associations.[3] Conversion therapy is both ineffective and damaging. Sexual fluidity is not subject to control; it occurs in unintentional and unexpected ways that cannot be harnessed or used to change fundamental sexual orientation. It can, however, occur spontaneously, be persistent, and result in life-long relationships, as I have found in my own forty-plus-year marriage.

I also interviewed two transgender men and a transgender woman. I wanted to gain more perspective into their experience, but it is so far outside my own and outside the scope of this book that I will only include ways in which our experiences parallel each other. Emma, a transgender woman, asks "What does it mean to be a woman? It's not just body parts or assigned sex. That question is a lot more complex than people think." My ninety-eight-year-old mother, in attempting to understand what transgender people may experience, talked about being a tomboy when she was little and wanting to do all the things boys were allowed to do. As we talked further, she understood the difference between a girl who wishes to be a boy and do "boy things," and a girl who feels a deep-down certainty that it simply feels wrong to be in a girl's body, moving through life as a girl. When my mom read the stories of people who feel their souls don't match their bodies, she began to feel compassion for a group of people she had not previously known. We have more to hear and understand from the experiences of our transgender spiritual siblings.

Regardless of how they identify, many of the women I talked to have a strong testimony of the Church. They often tell me they know the Book of Mormon came from God. They value their covenants. They feel a close connection to Jesus Christ and His gospel. But they also feel intense attractions to women, or perhaps just one woman, and they struggle to know what to do with that.

These women who are in and outside of marriages, or perhaps are dating women or married to women, and are at various stages of church engagement consistently assert this truth: God knows you and loves you. Connect with Heavenly Father. Keep praying. Stay close to God. God loves you as you are. He will help you find healing and comfort and compassion.

As I slowly began to open up to a few people, I was surprised at the stories I heard in return. I discovered I was not the only woman I knew who had felt attraction to a friend and found that at odds with their covenant, visible life. They may have never told the friend or anyone else, and it was a secret they held tightly hidden away. But I heard stories, some decades-old, that continued to fuel a bonfire of shame in their souls.

Is their attraction to women evidence of a hidden brokenness, they wonder, a fundamental flaw that will prevent them from finding happiness in this life and celestial glory with a family? They may be frightened by the disconnect between their life experience and their understanding of church doctrine. Many feel fierce allegiance to their covenant life but experience a constant internal dissonance and grief. Each of these women initially believed she was the only SSA woman who wanted to stay in the church; I assure you she is not. There is a way forward, and God is willing to be both guide and friend on that path.

As I come to know more Latter-day Saint women who find themselves somewhere on the scale of LGBTQ, I feel a sense of shared strength from other women who "get it" and who are able to offer advice from their experience and faith. I'm grateful I can share their voices with you. They are pioneers, striving to hear God's voice lead them through a wilderness with no paths carved out as yet but blazing trails that may help those behind them. Every time one of them opens up, comes out, and invites others in, she is putting out her hand to "succor the weak, lift up the hands which hang down, and strengthen the feeble knees" (D&C 81:5).

Notes for Chapter Two

1 Lisa M. Diamond, *Sexual Fluidity: Understanding Women's Love and Desire* (Cambridge, MA: Harvard University Press, 2009) 2–3.

2 Lisa M. Diamond, "Sexual Fluidity in Men and Women," *Current Controversies*, November 4, 2016, https://doi.org/https://psych.utah. edu/_resources/documents/people/diamond/Sexual%20Fluidity%20in%20 Males%20and%20Females.pdf.

3 "The Church of Jesus Christ of Latter-day Saints opposes 'conversion therapy' and our therapists do not practice it." (statement found at https://newsroom. churchofjesuschrist.org/article/statement-proposed-rule-sexual-orientation-gender-identity-change). It has also been discredited by the American Academy of Pediatrics, American College of Physicians, American Medical Association, and the American Psychiatric Association, and many others.

Chapter Three

LEARNING SELF-JUDGMENT

I attended Young Women's camp for the first time not long after I was baptized. I loved every minute of our time at the church camp up in the Sierra Nevada mountains of California. I was in a cabin with other twelve-year-old girls, and we had two "Big Sisters"—older girls who helped us learn the ropes of a camp with lots of traditions; coached us as we built four types of fires; and took us out to toss toilet paper into the trees of another group's campsite. It was an amazing week for me, and I had never felt so much love and acceptance.

At the end of the week, we had a testimony meeting. This was my first spiritual experience with friends my own age. At the end of the meeting, we each threw a pinecone into the fire, representing giving up a sin or bad habit to God. Then we sang "Each Campfire Lights Anew" during the Pinecone Ceremony. I was filled with the love of God and everyone around me.

As we finished, my Big Sister came up to me and hugged me. I remember standing, stiff as a board, my arms down at my side, thinking with horror, *My Big Sister is gay!* I had never been hugged by another girl. At my school, we had enormous personal space bubbles, and if anyone got within two feet, other girls would call out "Lezzie!" I didn't know exactly what that meant, but I knew it was bad—I still have to steel myself to say "Lesbian" because it feels like a swear word. I learned to avoid physical contact with other girls and to see any desire for it as shameful. It was the beginning of a long road of shame.

I joined the church about a year before that camp and junior high experience. I was reared as a Catholic. My mom was a Latter-day Saint but had not attended church since she was eighteen years old. She always came with us to our parish and even taught catechism. My mother woke up one morning hearing God tell her to get up and go to church, and she knew He didn't mean Mass. He wanted her to attend the Latter-day Saint church of her youth. A few weeks later, we all went with her. I liked the people and what I felt. The missionaries started teaching us, and I received everything I heard as truth. Here was God's presence, in my living room; I could feel Him as they taught. Later, kneeling by myself on my bedroom's shag carpet, I prayed to know if the Church was true. I felt a flood of warmth and light and joy fill me from my head down to my toes. I knew the truth, and I felt God call me to baptism and a new relationship with Him.

That relationship defines my life. He has called me into covenants with Him, and I treasure them. They bind me to Him. But as I grew older and I began to feel attraction to girls in my teenage years, I sensed an unresolvable tension between my covenant relationship with God and my interest in girls.

At that time, the language around homosexuality was harsh, and not just at school. Words like "abomination," "contamination," and "perversion" dominated the topic—in society, at Church, and in homes. There was no distinction made between feelings and actions, between attraction and covenant-breaking behavior. It was all sin. I determined there was no place for my feelings in the Church or in my relationship with God or in me, so I buried them under a mountain of denial and shame.

SATAN'S FIRST COMMANDMENT: HIDE

Hiding in shame kept me from going to God for truth about myself. I listened instead to my social and religious expectations, formed by the reactions and flawed opinions of the people around me. I was sure that God would reject me. To avoid that rejection, I never brought my full self to Him. Elder Dieter F. Uchtdorf states, "You are not invisible to your Heavenly Father. He loves you. He knows your humble heart."[1] If I had internalized that eternal truth in my youth, I might have learned love and acceptance for myself earlier.

Other women recount their varied reactions as they began to realize their feelings didn't align with what they were taught at home and church. Eliza says that every hour of every day she felt fear about being gay.

Jane had times when she would say to herself, "This is what I'm feeling, here's how I need to counter this so I won't do something God will punish me for." When she was fourteen and attracted to another girl, she wrote "NO NO NO NO NO" over and over in a journal to keep herself from thinking about it. She stayed as busy as she could with school and church so she "would not be sitting with [herself] and thinking about this."

Lolly was a terrified ten-year-old, sure that if her parents found out she was gay they wouldn't want to keep her. Wendy felt the same as a college freshman in Idaho, trying not to cry in the truck with her dad when he rolled down his window and yelled at two gay men walking down the street, using a homophobic insult and telling them to go back to California. A number of women described hearing gay slurs in their home growing up, and those casual comments that meant little to their families were daggers to their young hearts.

In contrast, Vanessa says she never experienced an identity crisis, and she's comfortable with the fact she's sometimes attracted to men, sometimes to women. It has not been an issue in her relationship with the church; she never felt it was a sin that she finds women attractive at times, and she never felt bad about having a crush. Growing up, she lived internationally, meeting people who were different in lots of ways. She felt that helped her to be more accepting and less judgmental and condemning about diversity. She was able to have that same acceptance for herself. Vanessa has always been at ease with her identity, but she seems to be in the minority.

Leila Jane says that when she got the green light to date around age sixteen, she realized "there are some boys I like and girls I like. The church says I can't date all of them; what will I choose here?" She found a case study of six gay Latter-day Saints, three who stayed in the church, and three who left. She observed that in this study, there was greater stability in staying in church, and she decided that was the path she would pursue. While it was a struggle learning to navigate her path into adulthood, her parents trusted her intuition in spite of their wariness.

The reality is that any home can have a gay child. What that child hears growing up can create a lifetime of self-loathing or it can teach them grace, acceptance, and kindness for themselves as well as others. Among the LGBTQ women I know, Vanessa and Leila Jane are exceptions. Their environment, both at home and with friends, helped them to feel self-acceptance and confidence as they recognized their attraction to women Without that positive environment, children fall back on immature coping strategies to help them navigate their profound dread of being rejected by God and the people they love, and those abandonment fears can carry forward for decades. Many of the women I interviewed struggle with deep-seated negative feelings about themselves based on what they internalized from their home and their communities, even if their behaviors are within Church standards. As they have matured, they have become better able to understand that God loves them exactly as they are, but it has taken many pain-filled years to get to that point of self-acceptance.

When we change the narrative in our homes, even without any alteration to Church policy or doctrine, it creates space for children to grow into a healthy self-image as they navigate the challenges of their sexuality within a gospel context. I recently heard a priesthood leader, speaking on the subject of LGBTQ inclusion, tell a group he was personally sorry for truths that may have been taught with vindictiveness, enmity, anger, or even well-intentioned ignorance. We can hold to the iron rod with a compassionate, kind grip. The more we love as the Savior did, the more we can create safe spaces for frightened children and others. When we know better, we can do better.

DENIAL: BOTH A FRIEND AND FOE

I grew up in a time before we knew better, and I am astonished at the magnitude of my denial for so many years. I saw but would not see. Somehow, I separated my obvious attraction to women from the conscious reality of my life, and I didn't challenge that fragmentation.

Denial is awesome and terrifying in its power. Melody Beattie describes it well:

> Denial is a protective device, a shock absorber for the soul. It prevents us from acknowledging reality *until* we feel prepared to cope with that particular reality. People can shout and scream the truth at us, but we will not see or hear it until we are ready.[2]

I averted my awareness away from my response to certain women because I was not ready to admit it. Even when I began to acknowledge a yearning, I thought of it as a desire for an affectionate, sisterly relationship. I have no sisters or aunts, and my mother loves me deeply but is not physically expressive. I've described my school years; obviously I didn't grow up in a culture where girls link arms with their friends as they walk, or cuddle on the couch while watching a movie. I see that among sisters, but I never experienced it. Could it be, I wondered, that I was just starved for healthy female affection? Denial continued, but at least I was opening a door and beginning to ask questions.

Until we are ready to "face reality," many of us categorize our pull to women as socially-acceptable admiration, deep friendship, charity, friendly affection, or intellectual connection. Others recognize that they are gay very early, around ten or eleven. They feel fundamentally different. At some point, all the women I interviewed had a moment of truth, often preceded by years of slowly increasing self-honesty. One common experience was watching a show, seeing two women characters connect romantically, and suddenly realizing it made sense and felt right in ways heterosexual romantic storylines never did.

Fear of the consequences can delay acknowledgement and acceptance. What will this mean for the future, for life plans, for covenants? It can be too much to take in all at once, but the underlying dread, shame, anxiety, and sadness are frequently there early on, pounding away inside.

I struggled from the time I was seventeen with periods of profound and, at times, suicidal depression. At one point when we had five young children and my husband was serving as bishop, I became convinced they would all be better off without me because I was not going to the celestial kingdom anyway. I would eventually be replaced, and why not now, when they could all have the benefit of a truly righteous wife and mother? Even though this was twenty years before I acknowledged my attraction to women, I felt so broken inside. I was afraid my brokenness would damage everyone around me. They all deserved better, I reasoned. When I read "It is better that one man perish than a nation dwindle in unbelief" during family scripture study, I was sure God was confirming my decision to end my mortal existence for the good of my family. Fortunately I was helped out of that suicidal period with therapy and medication. My husband was shocked and terrified at the thought of losing me, which challenged my false assumption that I was nothing more than a burden.

Looking back, I can see the relationship between waves of attraction for women that resulted in shame and fear, followed by a depressive episode. All of this was complicated by what I heard in my Church experience. The way Church leaders talk about LGBTQ members has shifted considerably in the past forty years, and quite a few of the general membership are following suit. Other members' attitudes and beliefs may lag behind, sometimes still stuck in the obsolete policies or traditions they were taught decades ago.

Almost ten years before I came out to myself, a non-member girl started attending my early-morning seminary class with one of her friends. She talked to me about her family—she is the daughter of a lesbian couple, and they were understandably concerned about her involvement with a conservative church that didn't seem to acknowledge the right of their family to exist. I remembered and shared with her President Gordon B. Hinckley's teaching from a conference address a few years before: "People inquire about our position on those who consider themselves . . . gays and lesbians. My response is that we love them as sons and daughters of God."[3] That was not something I had been taught twenty years before when I was a young adult. It was a softening of the harsh and condemning language I had heard as a young woman. As the conversation about same-sex attraction shifted, particularly in the church, I needed the protection of denial less and less. That shift was life-changing and life-saving for me.

INCREASED LIGHT AND KNOWLEDGE

The Restoration is ongoing, and we continue to learn more about God's children and how to respond to their varied experiences. Elder M. Russell Ballard states:

> There may be some doctrine, some policy, some bit of history that puts you at odds with your faith, and you may feel that the only way to resolve that inner turmoil right now is to "walk no more" with the Saints. If you live as long as I have, you will come to know that things have a way of resolving themselves. An inspired insight or revelation may shed new light on an issue. Remember, the Restoration is not an event, but it continues to unfold. [4]

When same-sex attraction was viewed as a choice, the expectations for how faithful Church members should react to those feelings was understandably grounded in the belief gay members were in open rebellion against God. The Church now teaches that same-sex attraction is *not* a choice. My feelings of relief were profound when I read this statement from Elder Ballard:

> Let us be clear: The Church of Jesus Christ of Latter-day Saints believes that "the experience of same-sex attraction is a complex reality for many people. . . . Even though individuals do not choose to have such attractions, they do choose how to respond to them."[5]

This paradigm shift changes the way leaders respond to LGBTQ members, the way teachers discuss same-sex attraction, and the way parents talk about gay people in front of their listening children (though cruelty was never okay). When we know better, we should do better. Understanding that same-sex attraction is not a choice alters it from being a rebellious sin to a reality I accept as part of who I am, a reality that deserves others' interest and empathy, not their condemnation. It shifts my focus to the real choice—choosing how I respond.

As a teenager, my options were stark: if I acknowledged my same-sex attraction, I felt there was no place in the Church for me. My friends who chose relationships with other girls left the church. I chose to stay, but I stayed with a lot of pain around how I perceived myself and with hidden feelings that were crushed by shame any time they started to bubble to the surface. Today, the language I hear at

Church is moving toward creating room for LGBTQ members to stay, with invitation for all members to rise to the challenge of creating a safe and loving space where everyone to worship. Elder Ballard shows us what this looks like:

> I want anyone who is a member of the Church who is gay or lesbian to know I believe you have a place in the kingdom and recognize that sometimes it may be difficult for you to see where you fit in the Lord's Church, but you do. We need to listen to and understand what our LGBT brothers and sisters are feeling and experiencing. Certainly, we must do better than we have done in the past so that all members feel they have a spiritual home where their brothers and sisters love them and where they have a place to worship and serve the Lord.[6]

We can let go of old ways of speaking and acting toward LGBTQ members and align our understanding with current teachings of General Authorities. What does that mean? It means we scoot over and make room on our pew. It means we open our hearts and minds and leave judgment to God and His appointed Judges in Israel. It means we are called to listen and learn and mourn and rejoice with each other. It means we offer sincere friendship.

I've seen this in action from my stake president, who is eager to inform himself about the needs of the LGBTQ members in his stake: he reads books, listens to podcasts, and ministers to LGBTQ members with an open heart and mind. He is invested in learning and sharing what he learns with the leaders and members of the stake. He doesn't dilute the teachings of the Church on chastity or marriage, but he finds space within those teachings to reach out to and love those who want to find a place in our community of faith. His heart is responding to the instruction from the General Handbook: "The Church encourages families and members to reach out with sensitivity, love, and respect to persons who are attracted to others of the same sex."[7] This invites discussion in our stake and unit councils, including the question "What does *reaching out* look like in our congregation?"

The Church's website states:

> God loves all of us. He loves those of different faiths and those without any faith. He loves those who suffer. He loves the rich and

poor alike. He loves people of every race and culture, the married or single, and those who experience same-sex attraction or identify as gay, lesbian, or bisexual. And God expects us to follow His example.[8]

These words shatter the expectations I created as a young woman. I believed that I was broken and unacceptable to God and to His covenant children. I couldn't release myself from my prison of fear and shame until there was a safe place of belonging where I could begin to come into the light. That safe space was created for me by the shifting attitudes in my home, my church, and my circle of friends. Today we each share a holy calling to be builders and curators of those safe spaces.

Notes for Chapter Three

1   Dieter F. Uchtdorf, "You Matter to Him," *Ensign,* November 2011.

2   Melody Beattie, "Letting Go of Denial," October 22, 2020, https://melodybeattie.com/letting-go-denial/.

3   Gordon B. Hinckley, "What Are People Asking about Us?" *Ensign*, November 1998.

4   M. Russell Ballard, "To Whom Shall We Go?" Ensign, November 2016.

5   M. Russell Ballard, "The Lord Needs You Now!" *Ensign*, September 2015.

6   M. Russell Ballard, "Questions and Answers," BYU Speeches, November 14, 2017, speeches.byu.edu.

7   *General Handbook: Serving in the Church of Jesus Christ of Latter-day Saints,* "Same-Sex Attraction and Same-Sex Behavior," 38.6.15, churchofjesuschrist.org.

8   "Does God Love Me?" https://www.churchofjesuschrist.org/study/manual/same-sex-attraction-individuals/does-god-love-me?lang=eng.

Chapter Four

A DELICATE BALANCING ACT

When you try a great recipe for Vegan Butter Chicken, the first impulse is to tell your friends! I did, and one of them suggested getting together to make an Indian lunch. The news spread, and soon we had a whole group of women who were going to bring Indian dishes, with the Butter Chicken as the main attraction. (In case you can't make sense of the paradoxical "Vegan Butter Chicken," it uses cauliflower instead of chicken and cashew cream instead of butter. It's amazing.)

We all gathered one day with friends bringing homemade naan, chana masala, palak paneer, and other favorites. The star of the show was the butter chicken, which I was demonstrating (there were a couple of tricky techniques involved). Everyone there was a friend, and most came from the institute class I taught Tuesday mornings for young moms—women who spent most of Sunday services out in the hall, in the nursery, or in the mother's lounge. Our institute class met in the Primary room with toys, so the small children could play, and the sisters didn't need to leave to nurse a baby or to take out a noisy child. We just talked a little louder while children played around us, and we could spend time with friends pondering the things of eternity. It was a safe space for discussing hard questions and a good spiritual and intellectual respite for these stressed-out young mothers. We formed close bonds of trust and friendship with each other. I felt so safe with them, yet I never shared my hidden secret of attraction to women.

Now I was in the kitchen with friends, sharing something I knew they would love, and yet as the minutes ticked past, I felt more and more isolated. When the food was prepared and we sat down to eat, I didn't know how to sit, or what to do with my hands. I felt out of place in my body, and I desperately wanted to leave. I didn't belong there. They were all good, righteous women. I felt broken in ways they couldn't understand, and I could never share. I was out of place with them and myself, and all I wanted to do was exit as quickly as possible. I felt comfortable in class every week because I could talk of the Atonement and testify of Christ. But here, alone, unprotected by that role as a witness of Jesus, I had to flee because I couldn't find my place. I felt the truth of Ann Morrow Lindbergh's observation that "if one is a stranger to oneself then one is estranged from others, too."[1]

Most LGBTQ women report feeling different as a child, even before puberty when their friends all started to like boys. They may have noticed they had different interests from other girls, or they just didn't feel at ease with the roles or expectations of a little girl—for dress, for behavior, or for relationships. It could have been hard for them to relate to friends who became focused on liking boys, dating, and dreaming of marriage to a man. Their attraction to some of those friends may have created shame and isolation. As adults, they may love the Lord and His gospel but have difficulty feeling that they fit into the Church roles and social framework that is expected of them. They often don't feel they really belong.

That experience might sound familiar. Many of us, gay or straight, are fragmented, teaching and testifying of truth, leading a consecrated life, while struggling with feelings of disconnection from ourselves as well as others. When I was still in denial, I lived with clashing personal tensions that created unhealthy internal and interpersonal dynamics. I was open and vulnerable one day and closed off and protective the next. I had everything most Latter-day Saint women want, and yet I was crippled by suicidal depression. I could be viewed as a role model and at the same time feel so broken and unworthy that I wanted to crawl away from interaction with any of the women in my ward. I inhabited a space in life that I valued, but I couldn't feel that I fit in it or deserved it.

MENTAL HEALTH EFFECTS

As Latter-day Saint women who experience same-sex attraction, we often endure anxiety, depression, and other debilitating responses to these conflicting realities. Years ago, I co-wrote a book called *Reaching for Hope: An LDS Perspective on Recovering from Depression.* We dove into the science and the story of clinical depression, including various triggers. Oddly enough, I never felt that I really understood the cause of my major depressive episodes. I finally decided it was postpartum depression. The hormonal effects of having babies and the subsequent sleep deprivation certainly were contributors, but that doesn't explain my bouts with depression before I had children.

Years later, after finally coming out of denial, I was able to connect the dots between waves of intense same-sex attraction and depressive episodes. During those times, I didn't have the skills or understanding to process what I was feeling, and so it channeled into and fueled a self-destructive mood disorder that expressed the darkness of my internal world. These bleak feelings about myself were reinforced by my mistaken views of God, both His nature and His expectations.

Many Latter-day Saint women feel overwhelmed by the impossibility of measuring up to what they believe God expects of them; that impossibility is magnified when you add romantic attraction to women in the mix. When River was twelve, she asked her brother what it means when someone is attracted to their own gender. His response was harsh and reflected his own struggles with SSA; he said that person would be better off killing himself and going to hell. Within a couple of weeks of talking to her brother, she stuck a loaded gun in her mouth with a finger on the trigger. She heard a voice saying, "Why would you reject the gift I've given you?" She put the gun down and went back to bed.

Sarah says that suicidal ideation (thinking about suicide) comes episodically, but death ideology (wishing to no longer be alive) is pervasive as an undercurrent in her life.

Blake, a successful professional woman, describes "wanting to be gone so badly." She cried first thing in the morning and cried herself to sleep at night.

Lolly believes that if she had come out at a younger age, her physical health would be much better. Shame and isolation intensify physical maladies in addition to depression, anxiety, and despair. When women begin to accept themselves and feel empathy and acceptance from others, it is powerfully healing.

At her lowest point, Lydia was afraid she might not have a full, bright future ahead of her, with a stable marriage. As she has come to understand herself and embrace who she is, she realizes her bisexuality isn't a threat to her happy life but a piece of her happy life.

In addition to self-acceptance, it's important to feel empathy and compassion from God. Before I came to that place, I had a consistent subtext of worthlessness running through my life, even as I wore myself out in God's service. I knew a lot about what He expected of me and very little of His grace.

In *The Gifts of Imperfection*, Brené Brown writes that we are worthy of both love and belonging. But when we judge any parts of ourselves "that don't fit in with who we think we're supposed to be, we stand outside of our story and hustle for our worthiness by constantly performing, perfecting, pleasing, and proving."[2] For Latter-day Saint women who experience same-sex attraction, there is often a deadly disconnect between who we are and who we think we need to be in order to deserve God's approval and the confidence of our loved ones.

The place I felt completely at peace was serving in the temple. That should have been an early clue that I was enough for God; in His most sacred space, I was at home. I felt it deeply when I served in Initiatory, that intimate space where women and the power of God come together in sublime ways. There were times when I felt I was a conduit for the love of God, sharing in that small area a sacred divine acceptance for our work and ourselves.

WHO AM I?

Outside the temple, I suffered a profound internal disconnection from myself and God. As I struggled with what Sheri Dew has called our "mortal identity crisis,"[3] I came across an unexpected book in the LDS bookstore near the Washington, D.C. Temple. It was called *Born That Way: A True Story of Overcoming Same-Sex Attraction with Insights for*

Friends, Families, and Leaders, by Laurie Campbell, writing under the pseudonym Erin Eldridge. I couldn't believe I was seeing a book on this topic published by Deseret Book! The subtitle gave me cover—I was buying this so I could be helpful if I ever had a gay friend. That was what I told my husband David, and that is what I told myself, because I was still unwilling to admit "the friend" could actually be me.

This was in 1994, and there were no welcoming arms, at least as far as I could see, for members of the church who were gay. Yet here was a book that took me into the mind and experience of an LDS gay woman. I had never seen anything like it. I consumed it, and I recommended it to others as "one of the best books I've ever read on the Atonement of Jesus Christ." That is true, but the larger story is that even then, in the midst of my denial, I found a woman whose experience resonated with me and gave me hope for a reconciliation between the opposing forces of same-sex attraction and devotion to Jesus Christ's Church.

All these decades later, I remember a paragraph that shaped the way I described myself from that point forward. Laurie writes, "Rather than saying I'm nothing without Jesus Christ, perhaps I should say that I am everything without Him: 'I am an alcoholic. I am a homosexual. I am a victim of sexual abuse.' The list goes on and on. But with Him, and because of Him, I am none of those things. I am a daughter of Christ."[4]

I tweaked her sentence and embraced the identity of "disciple of Christ." That became the truest expression of myself, the perfect summation of who I chose to become. When I would be introduced in one of my many roles—mother of so-and-so, President Decker's wife, the author of, the consultant for, or the called to serve as—always, always, I saw myself as primarily a disciple of Christ. That grounded me, even before I knew how my world would be turned topsy-turvy. That support was there when I thought I was going to spin out of control. And the grace I saw in Laurie's life gave me promise for my own. *Born that Way* gave me hope before I acknowledged how desperately I would need it. Much later, right after coming out to myself and David, I saw Laurie's video on the church website, and I reached out to her. She responded to me as she has so many others, with graciousness and generosity.

The next twenty years were characterized by mothering my growing children, serving in the Church, holding myself together, and surviving the waves of unacknowledged attraction.

In college, with amazing roommates who were beautiful and wonderful women, I had unconsciously managed friendships through strengthening spiritual connection. Consecrating the loving feelings I have for women enables me to have close and fulfilling friendships—most of the time—unless the dissonance becomes too great, and I simply have to step away. But on a day-to-day basis, I gravitate toward intense spiritual conversations rather than superficial friendships and arts-and-crafts discussions. I'm sure I have appeared deeply religious to everyone, especially my children. What they don't see is that this connection to God is the only way for me to thrive in the life I choose. My coping mechanism, even before I came out to myself, was to try to move relationships onto a spiritual plane, shifting my own feelings from natural to transcendent.

Years later, my therapist introduced me to the Domains of Attraction (see diagram on the next page), which describe the types and degrees of opposite-sex and same-sex attraction. Most people experience some degree of same-sex attraction, although for people who identify as heterosexual these attractions are primarily aesthetic ("I love her haircut!") or affectional (the love we have for friends, or women we serve with as a presidency). Since most people land somewhere on a spectrum of same- or opposite-sex attraction, it's helpful to examine different types and degrees of attraction. The domains consist of Aesthetic, Affectional, Romantic, and Erotic. My therapist adds in Spiritual, which resonates with me; I know I often feel a strong spiritual attraction to people. I would place "Spiritual" at the top of the page because it can infuse all domains and degrees of attraction.

Domains of Attraction[5]

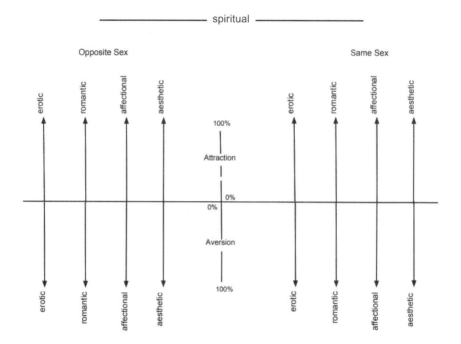

I believe that the shift from affectional or spiritual to romantic is not necessarily a movement from good to evil; those romantic feelings may not be innately bad, but acting on them is outside bounds set by the Lord. Loving others, including romantic love, is inherently good. But if that love takes me outside my covenants, it becomes wrong to me.[6] Elder M. Russell Ballard encourages parents to be "positive about how wonderful and beautiful physical intimacy can be when it happens within the boundaries the Lord has set, including temple covenants and commitments of eternal marriage."[7] I find it fascinating that we talk about chastity with boundary language. Many women talk about how confused they are by their feelings for other women, because it doesn't feel wrong; rather, it seems good and natural. When I consider a relationship with a woman as prohibited instead of inherently evil, it makes more sense to me. That also makes it easier for me to work on moving my feelings from romantic to spiritual because shame and fear don't get in the way.

I experienced times of attraction to the women I served, even when I was working to keep my feelings in a spiritual or affectional domain. That was when my fragmentation became most pronounced. I didn't have the framework at the time to understand different domains of attraction, boundaries, or moving into transcendent spaces. All of this language and understanding came later. I just vaguely knew that I was thinking too much about another woman. That awareness was enough to drive me into shame and hopelessness and depression. My identity as a disciple of Christ was at odds with my feelings about myself and others, and I began to feel more and more emotionally unstable. When I felt that things were moving to a breaking point, it was actually the beginning of my healing.

Notes for Chapter Four

1   Ann Morrow Lindbergh, *Gift from the Sea* (NY, NY: Random House, 2005).

2   Brené Brown, *Gifts of Imperfection* (Center City, MN: Hazelden Publishing, 2010).

3   Sheri Dew, *No Doubt About It* (Salt Lake City, UT: Bookcraft Pubs, 2002).

4   Erin Eldridge, *Born that Way?: A True Story of Overcoming Same-sex Attraction with Insights for Friends, Families, and Leaders* (Salt Lake City, UT: Deseret Book, 1994), 128–129.

5   A. Lee Beckstead, *Can we change sexual orientation?* Archives of Sexual Behavior, 41(1) (2012): 121–34.

6   As I try to understand this for myself, I call to mind President Dallin H. Oaks' description of a distinction in law: "Some acts, like murder, are crimes because they are inherently wrong. Other acts, like operating without a license, are crimes only because they are legally prohibited. Under these distinctions, the act that produced the Fall was not a sin—inherently wrong—but a transgression—wrong because it was formally prohibited." I don't want to wrest President Oaks' meaning out of context, but could that be the reason there is not a vast gulf between affectional and romantic? Could it be wrong by prohibition, rather than inherently evil? When I pondered that possibility, it became easier to accept my attractions and love for women, which doesn't *feel* wrong, while also reminding myself that acting on those feelings would take me out of my integrity and the boundaries I accept as my own from God.

7   M. Russell Ballard, "Fathers and Sons: A Remarkable Relationship," *Ensign,* November 2009.

Chapter Five

SHAME IS THE REAL ENEMY

One Sunday morning, shortly after telling David about my attraction to women, I was teaching Sunday School. When our Gospel Doctrine class ended, a sister came up to talk to me. She enthusiastically complimented me on the discussion. As she looked at me with admiration and told me I was an inspiring teacher, I interrupted her to say, vehemently, "I'm broken. We are all broken and in need of a Savior." She looked at me with a puzzled expression; my reply did not follow the usual script of a compliment followed by an appreciative but humble response. I knew it was off, but how could I say what I was really thinking? *You don't know me. If you really knew me, you wouldn't say that.*

For years, those words or some variation replayed in my mind every time people offered kind words to me in response to my talks, workshop presentations, lessons, or a new calling or release. One of my institute students, a young mom, told me she wanted to be like me. Her words, meant to make me feel good, were like a knife in my heart. The gap between how she saw me and what I thought of myself was excruciatingly painful.

Appreciative words bounced off my walls of shame. Deep down I felt certain that my fatal flaw of same-sex attraction would override any good I accomplished. The shame that I felt, even when it was vague and shadowy in the years before I came out to myself, defined my self-perception. I was sure others, including my friends and family, would be disgusted if they knew my whole truth. This condemnation admitted no defense or mercy; I weighed myself in the balance and came up lacking.

My shame was rooted in the romantic attractions I felt, but shame can grow in our lives from all sorts of seeds. We learn it young, and we learn it hard, especially women. A couple of years ago I was asked to teach a workshop on shame at Young Women's camp. As I prepared, I thought about the questions I would ask and whether the girls would be comfortable in answering them. Their ages ranged from seventeen down to twelve years old. Would they even have the life experience to know what I was talking about?

One of those questions was "Where in your body do you feel shame?" I anticipated that the response would be silence. Even if these young girls had the glimmer of an answer, who would feel safe enough to respond to the question in front of her friends?

After some introductory stories, I asked them the question I intended and let the thought hang there for a few moments. I planned to continue by explaining we can have a physical response to shame and share examples. I was pretty sure we could get past the discomfort and confusion and introduce some new ideas to these girls.

But I underestimated their acquaintance with this cruel companion. They all knew shame and could describe its physical sensations in detail. One felt shame in her throat, as it would tighten and constrict her breathing. Another felt sick to her stomach. A young girl described a crushing feeling in her chest, and the girl next to her talked about an instant tightening in her neck and shoulders and a headache.

I didn't have to introduce shame; it was a part of their everyday existence, and they were eager to share what they knew. It was an eye-opening and deeply sad moment for me. I see the same thing in adult women: if I ask them to think about that one thing they don't want anyone to know about, I see the fear in their eyes. We know shame. Sadly, we generally don't outgrow it.

As an adult, Sky says her biggest challenge is shame. "Sometimes I get too close to a woman, and that's confusing because it feels so much like home," she explains. She tries to be "super careful about boundaries," but her heartache is sometimes unbearable when she dwells on the fear that she's going to be alone forever.

Many of us recognize that feeling of disconnection from others, the unworthiness, the profound sense of not being right that accompanies shame. Brené Brown researches and writes about shame, and her work has helped many begin to push back against this soul-crushing demon. She defines shame as "the intensely painful feeling or experience of believing we are flawed and therefore unworthy of acceptance and belonging. . . . Shame creates feelings of fear, blame and disconnection."[1] She explains that shame grows best in the environment of secrecy, silence, and self-judgment.

Why is shame universal? Where do we learn it? Our society often uses it as a teaching tool: "Don't pick your nose, that's disgusting" to a two-year-old; "Don't wear clothes that give boys bad thoughts" to our teenage girls; "Mom, don't wear those pants, they look dumb" from our kids. Shame can be used to manipulate others (for their own good, we tell ourselves). Sometimes we use it to try to motivate ourselves to change our habits. But shame is not a good motivator. It makes us feel defeated, not inspired. Shame kills hope.

SHAME DOES NOT COME FROM GOD

Shame is evident as a tool of the adversary in this scripture: "And I heard a loud voice saying in heaven, Now is come salvation, and strength, and the kingdom of our God, and the power of his Christ: for the accuser of our brethren is cast down, which accused them before our God day and night" (Revelation 12:10-11).

I know that accusing voice. I have internalized it and believed it. This information in the New Testament Student Manual for institute classes helped me begin to recognize and reject those accusations:

> The name-title "Satan" comes from a Hebrew verb meaning "to accuse," "to slander," or "to be an adversary." Thus, the title "accuser" (Revelation 12:10) reflects Satan's efforts as the adversary of the human family, charging people with sin. Elder Dieter F. Uchtdorf of the Quorum of the Twelve Apostles discussed Satan's title of "accuser": "The scriptures call him the 'accuser' because he wants us to feel that we are beyond forgiveness (see Revelation 12:10). Satan wants us to think that when we have sinned we have gone past a 'point of no return'—that it is too late to change our course".[2] The

phrase "day and night" (Revelation 12:10) reinforces that Satan does not cease his effort to destroy the disciples of Jesus Christ.[3]

The voice of the accuser has accused me day and night, but not before a judge as gentle as our God; he has accused me to myself, where he found a jury eager to convict and a judge quick to condemn. Convincing me of my own worthlessness is a perfect way to stop my progression and destroy my hope.

I didn't acknowledge or admit my attraction to women until after my children were adults, even though that attraction to girls started when I was a teenager. I was in denial for years, but shame still oozed into all the crevices of my life, and when my children were young, I found myself convinced that my husband and children would be better off without me.

I had moved beyond shame and into a suicidal depression. Loving voices, medication, and counseling diminished the depression that almost killed me. Cognitive Behavioral Therapy enabled me to recognize and reject distorted thinking. Yet shame still hung on; it was the soundtrack of my life for many more years.

The twelfth chapter of Revelation teaches the difference between God's voice and the voice of the accuser. It is easy to listen to the constant, deafening voice of shame. It takes effort to turn to God and invite His quiet and loving voice instead. In Revelations 12:11 we are shown how the children of God can reject the power of the accuser's voice: "They overcame him by the blood of the Lamb, and by the word of their testimonies." My witness of the Atonement of Jesus Christ is more powerful than the lies of the adversary.

Elder Neal A. Maxwell taught:

[Many] of us who would not chastise a neighbor for his frailties have a field day with our own. Some of us stand before no harsher a judge than ourselves . . . Fortunately, the Lord loves us [much] more than we love ourselves. What can we do to manage these vexing feelings of inadequacy? We can distinguish more clearly between . . . dissatisfaction with self and disdain for self. We need the first and must shun the second. He who was thrust down in the first estate delights to have us put ourselves down. Self-contempt is of Satan; there is none of it in heaven.[4]

God may show me my sins, but it is always combined with hope in Christ, the assurance that I can change and do better, and the invitation to come to Him and be healed. The accuser offers no hope, only despair. *This* is my measure, the rule by which I decide whether or not to listen: If the awareness of my failings comes with hope in Christ, I turn to Him and listen. If shame tells me instead that I will never be good enough, I am not worthy, I am too broken to be fixed, and God's grace is not meant for "such as I"—I know that Satanic voice. He is a liar from the beginning, and I refuse to listen anymore.

HEARING GOD'S VOICE

I delight to listen to the voice of God now, even when I am doing wrong. There is a thrill that comes with self-honesty and owning my mistakes. His gentle voice invites me back into His light and truth. He desires to heal me. The more I learn of God, the more I love Him. It is His love that draws me away from sin, not my fear of Him or His punishments. I feel the truth of Elder Richard G. Scott's description: "By understanding the Atonement, you will see that God is not a jealous being who delights in persecuting those who misstep. He is an absolutely perfect, compassionate, understanding, patient, and forgiving Father. He is willing to entreat, counsel, strengthen, lift and fortify.⁵"

Knowing the true nature of God is essential to rejecting the accuser's lying voice and recognizing the loving and encouraging voice of our Father. In *Lectures on Faith,* Joseph Smith teaches us about the essential attributes of faith and the importance of understanding the nature of God:

> Three things are necessary, in order that any rational and intelligent being may exercise faith in God unto life and salvation. First, The idea that he actually exists. Secondly, A *correct* understanding of his character, perfections, and attributes. Thirdly, An actual knowledge that the course of life which he is pursuing, is according to his will.[6]

I have always believed God exists. But because I believed in a God who would not listen to my prayers if I said them in bed instead of on my knees, who would be angry at me when I lost patience with my kids, or who would withdraw from me when I needed him the most, I had built up an idol in the image of man. I didn't begin to truly know God until I learned through my own experience of His love, His patience, His tenderness, and His mercy.

While visiting one of my daughters in Utah, I wanted to do some temple work for our family. We had a limited amount of time, and the youth in her ward who were scheduled to do the baptisms for us ended up not going. I asked my daughter if we could swing by the Mount Timpanogos Utah Temple on our way home from an activity with her little kids. I intended to ask at the temple if they could add my family file when youth groups came in to do baptisms that afternoon. We could then return in the evening during our babysitter window of time to do the remainder of the work.

I was dressed for an outing with grandchildren, not temple attendance. To my surprise, the workers did more than just accept my family file cards. I was invited to come into the baptistry and watch the proxy baptisms. I walked in, past many white-clothed temple workers (there are a lot of temple workers in Utah!). I watched the baptisms, and during one for a near relative, I had a powerful spiritual experience. I felt her eagerness to accept the ordinance and the importance of my being there to share the moment with her. Even as I sat there in jeans, tennis shoes, and an olive-drab jacket, I felt God's love for me and for my family. I was then invited into the confirmation room, where I experienced the same thing. Nothing but love, acceptance, and kindness from God and reflected from each temple worker. The brothers thanked me for coming, and the sisters smiled at me on my way in and my way out. I expected at least a few side-eyes. My expectation was that I was not "appropriately" dressed to be there. They looked past all of that to my heart, and they loved me for my good intent. God does the same, even when my soul comes before him in jeans, tennis shoes, and olive drab.

I have heard that people don't break our hearts, they break our expectations. My expectations about myself and the expectations I imposed on myself from God (without much of His input) broke my heart. Those expectations were destructive and damning until I gained the perspective to challenge and replace them. My attraction to women was never the damaging issue; for most of those years, I didn't even allow myself to acknowledge it. The shame I felt in response to that buried attraction did the greatest damage.

When I assumed that friend who complimented my Sunday School lesson would reject me if she knew the truth about me, I did her a disservice. Later, she was one of the first people I opened up to about my attraction to women. She was not rejecting or even surprised. When I was in emotional pain, she had perceived through the Spirit what was hurting me. She continued to enjoy my Sunday School class and stayed my dear friend, patiently giving me time and space to decide if I ever wanted to confide in her. Her acceptance and love taught me about true disciples who reflect the image of a loving God in their countenance. When I felt the compassion and empathy of the Lord and my friends, I was able to step out of the secrecy, silence, and self-judgment that kept me in a prison of shame.

Notes for Chapter Five

1   Brené Brown, *I Thought it was Just Me (But It Isn't): Women Reclaiming Power and Courage in a Culture of Shame* (New York, NY: Gotham, 2007), 5.

2   Dieter F. Uchtdorf, "Point of Safe Return," *Ensign*, May 2007, 99.

3   "Revelation 12–16," *New Testament Student Manual*, Church Educational System manual, 2014.

4   Neal A. Maxwell, "Notwithstanding My Weakness," *Ensign*, November 1976.

5   Richard G. Scott, "Finding Forgiveness." *Ensign*, May 1995.

6   Joseph Smith, *Lectures on Faith*, quoted in "Lectures on Theology ('Lectures on Faith')" Church History Topics, churchofjesuschrist.org.

Chapter Six

RECKONING AND
AUTHENTICITY

After a lifetime of suppression and denial, I found myself one day thinking about a friend, wondering if—and hoping—she was gay. I stood up, walked into the bathroom, looked in the mirror, and said out loud "It's time to admit you're attracted to women."

What broke the barrier? Nothing dramatic other than one more very clear evidence that I didn't think about women the way straight women think about women. At this point all my children were grown and out of the house. I had less stress and more contemplative time. I was serving in a less demanding calling, and I was able to handle a reality that would have been overwhelming a few years before. I was becoming more aware of LGBTQ topics, characters in movies, and news stories. I also think that God knew I was ready to grow, and so He gave me strength to let go of my self-protection and face a reality that I couldn't previously. Melody Beattie explains that denial "refers to our ability to ignore what is happening, even when it is right before our eyes. We do this to protect ourselves until we are ready to face the truth."[1]

Even though I had not yet acknowledged same-sex attraction, I had been in therapy for depression, and I had developed much healthier ways of thinking and coping as a result. I was also involved in Twelve Step programs, which helped me to increase my trust in God and my ability to be honest with myself. I had a group of supportive, non-judgmental friends. David and I were in a good place in our marriage. All of these positive components created a safe framework for me to become honest with myself about something that terrified me. At the time, I didn't think ahead, didn't ask all the "What does this mean for my life?" questions. I just allowed myself to sit with the reality of what I had finally acknowledged.

That quiet sitting lasted a few weeks until God asked of me the hardest sacrifice of my life—He asked me to tell David. I don't know how long I struggled with that request. I remember sobbing on my hands and knees, begging that he would not require it of me. What I received was a gentle, persistent invitation to tell my husband. I intended to take this secret to the grave, and God was asking me to tell the person I most wanted to shield from the pain of revelation.

Eventually, I decided to trust God. Even now, I don't know where the willingness came from. Maybe a hope that if God was so insistent, it would have a good result? Perhaps He just wore me down. I realized I couldn't be at peace until I did as He asked, and I turned over the outcome to Him.

That year on Christmas Eve, David and I were alone. Our kids were all elsewhere for the holidays, and we were sitting on the floor in front of our tree, leaning against the couch and enjoying being together. I was aware that at that point we were in one of the best moments of our marriage. We were at ease together, our kids were in a good place (even though they weren't with us), and our life felt happy and content. All of that gave me courage to speak to him; I felt that this moment was filled with safety and love and good feeling, and that was the environment I needed. I told him I wanted to share something about myself, and then I said, "I am attracted to women."

This conversation took place eight years ago. If I were doing it today, I would do so much better. I would immediately assure him that I love him, that I don't want to change my life, that I chose him years ago and continue to choose him. I would talk to him about what I thought this meant for my life and our life, and I would reassure him of my commitment to my covenants with God and my relationship with him.

But I didn't know to say all those things. I learned all of that through experience—experience I lacked at the time. I didn't realize where his fear would take him, and I didn't tell him all the things he needed to hear. I gave him the facts, without any context. At one point he said, "Maybe you should go visit one of our daughters for a few weeks." I heard rejection rather than his fear and pain. I decided that the best place for me was at home, where we could try to work on this together.

A couple of days later, one of our daughters in Utah experienced a serious, life-threatening medical event, and I had to leave. As I rode the train from the airport to her apartment, I listened over and over to a song from Rob Gardner's *Lamb of God,* an oratorio that depicts the last week of the Savior's life, His death, and resurrection. Thomas' song "Sometime We'll Understand" expressed the confusion, agony, and hope of my heart:

> Not now, but in the coming years,
> It may not be when we demand,
> We'll read the meaning of our tears,
> And there, sometime, we'll understand
>
> Why what we long for most of all
> Eludes our open, pleading hand;
> Why ever silence meets our call,
> Somewhere, sometime, we'll understand.
>
> So trust in God through all thy days;
> Fear not, for He doth hold thy hand;
> Though dark thy way, still sing and praise,
> Sometime, sometime we'll understand.[2]

I listened to that song on a continuous loop as the landscape flashed past outside the train windows, and I wondered what I had done to my life. Was I going to find any meaning for my tears and the pain I inflicted on my husband? Why was God demanding blind trust from me without showing me the way forward? What would happen when I went home? Would I be able to go home? And what did I really want, after all? How would this revelation change my life, either through shutting doors or opening new ones?

THE WRESTLE AND THE ROLLER COASTER

Over the next few weeks, as my daughter's condition improved, then worsened, then gradually improved again, I wrestled with God. I stayed awake at night on my blow-up mattress behind the couch reading Diamond's *Sexual Fluidity* on my iPad. I went for long walks while my daughter rested, and I railed at God. I started swearing for the first time in my life—swearing at Him. I felt so unmoored from the life I had always known that as I walked by Starbucks, I wondered if I was going to start drinking coffee next.

I felt disconnected from who and what I was, and I didn't know what I would choose or what my options would be. I knew that I wanted to stay in my marriage, but what *should* I do? Was that living a lie and unfair to David? My life had been so scripted and clear—covenants, marriage, family, service—but nothing in my current experience was on the Latter-day-Saint-woman road map. I fell off the edge of the map, and I didn't know if my life with David was a heartfelt commitment to him or a betrayal of both of us. Now that I had thrown a bomb into my life, what next? What did God want from me? My journal entries capture the roller-coaster feeling of that time:

December 2013 to February 2014

I don't want to be alone, and I dread being with people. I want to hide, and I'm afraid of being unseen. I feel like I'm in a nightmare and that every direction I turn to offers no relief, only pain. Existence is a burden, but the thought of hurting people I love is terrifying. I want to turn to God, but my mind can't rest and settle and feel peace.

What does He want from me? Is this a prompting or my disordered mind making things even worse than they are? . . .

. . . So I jumped off the cliff. I told David about my SSA issues. I also told him I have never done anything that violated my covenants. I have always been faithful to them. I love him, and I'm attracted to him—but I also have these other thoughts and feelings that intrude into my mind, and which I have had to deal with off and on through my life.

I felt peace once I decided to talk to David. I think this could go either way—it could destroy our relationship or make it stronger than it has ever been. We certainly can't just maintain the status quo.

But I wonder what else God wants me to do. So much of the SSA/Mormon issue is based on the assumption that people can't live happily in a mixed orientation marriage. We don't have that—I am attracted to David—but we do have a situation where I can be attracted to women at church or at the grocery store, and I have to deal with those feelings, while at the same time being in a happy and faithful marriage and staying worthy to serve at church. . . .

. . . This has been so hard on David. Yesterday he mentioned again that before I talk to anyone else about this I should talk to the stake president—and that he (David) might be released as his counselor. I was shocked that he said that. I don't think that would be true, but I am so sorry and sad that he even thought it.

His neck and shoulder have been hurting. I'm sure it's because of this. We've talked a lot, but it's still building up inside of him. I was scared last night. He seemed so much more distant. I think I recognized cognitively that this could really damage our marriage, but emotionally I didn't believe it. I see and feel now that it could have long-lasting repercussions, and that even if we end up stronger, it's going to be difficult before that.

I was so relieved the last two days; now the fear and regret are setting in. . . .

. . . I'm sorry for making David feel so terrible, and I feel guilty, but I also feel relief for being seen. Sometimes I think this is a big deal over nothing, and then I feel it is something that threatens my physical and spiritual existence, and it could bring destruction to people I love.

I know I'm numbing out because I'm so afraid of the weight of shame and guilt and sorrow. But it also numbs me to joy and peace and happiness, and I'm afraid to talk to the Lord. I rehearse things in my mind, but I don't want to talk to Him.

I realized today that I only said the words to myself a few weeks ago—that seems so silly, but really it was the first moment of actually admitting and accepting this, even though it's always been part of my life, pushed away or ignored or hidden. Now that I've admitted it to myself, I feel like the ground is shaking, and I'm not sure how to find my balance. . . .

. . . I want to find that balance with the Lord. I want to turn to Him, but I feel like I'm still hiding, turning my face away from

Him, hoping he won't be able to see me if I'm not looking at Him.

I've read some conference talks and scriptures, and I've been singing some hymns, but I don't feel a desperate desire, and I'm not getting much back. I did read this quote from Elder Uchtdorf today: "Lift up your soul in prayer and explain to your Heavenly Father what you are feeling. Acknowledge your shortcomings. Pour out your heart and express your gratitude. Let Him know of the trials you are facing. Plead with Him in Christ's name for strength and support. Ask that your ears may be opened, that you may hear His voice."[3] . . .

. . . In the last few days I've felt that same desire to break down and just be bad. I feel disconnected from God, and I realize it's all on my end, but I'm not desperate to repair the breach. Just trying to figure out who and what I really am. I feel so confused. Should I think about my Sunday School lesson? Ways to die? Whether to drink coffee? What those people are thinking that I pass in the store? I don't feel the Spirit, and nothing is clear or makes sense. But I know the people around me will suffer for my sins, and I love them. Why can't I feel connected to my feelings, to reality?

Jen sent me a message today that calmed me: "Maybe taking the pressure off of yourself to figure this out and instead trusting that the Lord will provide the peace that you desire as you put one foot in front of the other. Try not to judge your feelings. Accept them. Love yourself. All of yourself. Love you, Jen" . . .

. . . I want to go into a cave and hide. With David. He is safety for me, he and God, and everything else is scary and stupid and threatening and full of expectations that I will be someone I'm not. I hate how I feel. I want to go back to David, but nothing else. Even in the Draper temple last week, I heaved a sigh of relief, thinking that no one there knew me—then I saw my next-door neighbor from high school. I can run, but I can't hide, apparently.

I wrote an email today, basically begging to be released as seminary & institute supervisor without actually asking. I don't want anyone to expect anything from me. Except to take care of my kids. I can do that. And David. I miss David, but I'm glad to be here with [our daughter]. I just wish he were here, too, and we could go for a walk, and I could lean against his chest and cry.

[Later, at home in Michigan,] David just left to go snowshoeing. I think I've underestimated the emotional turmoil he's feeling.

As I am starting to feel better, David is starting to feel worse. He came home, ate dinner, and went out to walk through the woods in the dark. He's trying to sort out his emotions, I think, and they're confusing. This is a mess. I hope it's the mess the Lord is intending to work with, and not just one I've created to hurt without any value.

BUILDING SAFETY AND TRUST

Growth is scary and messy and confusing. David and I would have benefitted from counseling during this period, but that didn't come for another six years. We tried to find our own way through it: we worked through a Gottman Institute video/workbook program, we read books, and I think almost every talk David delivered in stake conferences and unit conferences had something to do with relationships. We resolved some long-standing issues and negative patterns in our communication. I remember at one time telling him that I couldn't keep doing this, that our relationship had to change because neither of us was happy. At that point I knew we would either need to change or break up—not because I was attracted to women but because we didn't have a relationship where we both felt safe and nurtured.

That was a turning point for me. I didn't want to stay guarded and distant anymore. We talked about what made us both feel unsafe and what needed to change. My critical words and David's withdrawal were devolving into a negative spiral for our relationship. We had both been hiding feelings from each other because we thought they would only do damage and hurt the other person, but we were actually each becoming avoidant, which could have been a death knell for our marriage.

When we committed to more honesty, even about things that could be hurtful to the other, we started to engage in healthier ways. Walls of self-protection and well-intentioned but damaging efforts to protect each other started to come down. We talked about our thoughts and feelings more, rather than just the business of the family. Gradually years of relationship habits shifted, and we started to get to know each other better. I'm grateful David was willing to stay committed to me and our marriage and do the hard work. I wasn't sure what God had for me and us at the bottom of the cliff, but I'm glad I closed my eyes and took the leap.

I read several talks by Elder Richard G. Scott during this time, and I always received understanding, compassion, and good counsel. He says:

> When you pass through trials for His purposes, as you trust Him, exercise faith in Him, He will help you. That support will generally come step by step, a portion at a time. While you are passing through each phase, the pain and difficulty that comes from being enlarged will continue. If all matters were immediately resolved at your first petition, you could not grow. Your Father in Heaven and His Beloved Son love you perfectly. They would not require you to experience a moment more of difficulty than is absolutely needed for your personal benefit or for that of those you love.[4]

Now, with the perspective of years and retrospection, I see that what Heavenly Father offered me was growth, one painful step at a time: my growth, David's growth, our marriage's growth and our family's growth. We are not the people we were; we are better. We know more about how God works with His children, and I see my husband reflecting that new understanding in the way he responds to me.

We have increased authenticity in our relationship. I had been hiding from myself and from him for our whole marriage. Neither of us felt safe and open. One of the stark examples of this constant hiding was my refusal to take general anesthesia. I knew that coming out of anesthesia, I would not be in complete control of what I said—what if I thought the nurse was cute? What might I say in front of David? Even unconsciously in my state of denial, I couldn't take that risk, and so I talked doctors into forgoing general anesthesia for procedures and surgeries that would normally require it. I explained that my dad has a terrible reaction to anesthesia, and I didn't want to risk it. They either used locals or nothing. My doctors thought I was a rock star. Hey, I can handle pain—physical pain was nothing compared to the pain of revealing myself.

That iron grip turned into an iron curtain in my marriage. I would allow just so much vulnerability and honesty, and no more. It was the same in friendships, with my parents and, most damaging, with God. I could pray for help with planning stake YW camp or a seminary lesson. But help with my attraction to women? We simply never talked about it.

After revealing myself to David, the next few years taught me the truth that vulnerability invites intimacy. Honesty, openness, and trust became a part of our relationship in a new way. He was able to receive my truth without being overwhelmed by his own fears and suspicion. I began to feel relief as I relaxed the iron grip on myself. I had held myself so tightly and fearfully. It took time to let go of that. There were new tensions, to be sure, but they were the result of honesty and openness. We can each retreat into hurt and loneliness, but we spend less and less time there. Light and truth began to gradually transform our relationship, with my willingness to let him see more of me and his growing willingness to see and accept me and allow me to see more of him, as well.

EACH PATH IS UNIQUE

Once again, this is my particular journey; I know other women who have made different choices and many who had different options, depending on their husbands' reactions. Some relationships don't survive, and some spouses can't overcome the pain and uncertainty. But I have observed positive results in the marriages of several of the women I interviewed. Mariah was isolating, choosing not to connect to women to protect her marriage and family, but her husband sensed the lack of connection, too. She felt like she was in a fog, hiding in a very stoic life and never fully alive. Coming out as a gay woman strengthened her marriage and improved her connection to other women and her husband.

Wally recognized that if she wasn't completely honest with herself or her husband, she would keep operating from shame. She knew that if she was going to continue in the church and her marriage, she had to be 100% authentic. She felt whisperings in conversations with Heavenly Father. The Spirit led her to a feeling of peace that she could talk to her husband, and it would be okay. She received personal revelation that it would not be easy, but if she was willing to let the mess in, it would mean incredible things for other people and her family. She affirms that "If you're true to yourself it will mean miracles."

The Savior promises that as we act on His words, "ye shall know the truth, and the truth shall set you free" (John 8:32). He led me into truth about myself and shared truth with my husband, and it set both of us free from years of fear, constraint, and hiding. We are growing into a new and better place.

Notes for Chapter Six

1   Melody Beattie, *Codependents' Guide to the Twelve Steps: How to Find the Right Program for You and Apply Each of the Twelve Steps to Your Own Issues* (New York, NY: Simon & Schuster, 2002).

2   Rob Gardner, "Sometime We'll Understand," *Lamb of God,* Rob Gardner Music (2012); adapted from original text written by Maxwell Cornelius (1842-1893).

3   Dieter F. Uchtdorf, "The Hope of God's Light," *Ensign,* May 2013.

4   Richard G. Scott, "Trust in the Lord," *Ensign,* November 1995.

Chapter Seven

WHERE DO WE GO
FROM HERE?

Following that Christmas Eve of 2013, both David and I wanted to know where I fit on the scale of sexual orientation. Was I lesbian? Bisexual? That was what drove me to read *Sexual Fluidity* as the first of many books. Dr. Diamond describes the fluid nature of some women's sexual attractions. She explains a woman "might experience her new-found . . . attractions as long-lasting if the relationship develops into a stable, long-term bond. Alternatively, the attractions might disappear altogether if the relationship dissolves. The key point is that the attractions triggered by fluidity do not alter a woman's basic orientation, though they might function like an orientation in terms of consistency."[1]

Women in her study often describe themselves as falling in love with a person, not a gender. Diamond explains "virtually all the women with person-based attractions agreed strongly with the statement, 'When I'm really emotionally bonded to someone, I find myself becoming physically attracted to them.'"[2] This helped me to understand that my attraction to David was real and legitimate, not something I had constructed to fit religious and social expectations. I could trust in it, even though it seemed misaligned with my basic orientation.

I learned that some women experience attraction to other women on a consistent basis, with no glimmer of attraction to men. Others feel drawn to both men and women, in varying degrees. Some women are surprised to find they are beginning to feel romantic attraction toward their best friend, even though they have never experienced same-sex attraction before. Another group of women who felt they were firmly on the lesbian end of the spectrum may discover attraction and marriage to a particular man works for them, while others who have tried heterosexual relationships have found only pain and anguish as a result.

My main takeaway was that though my sexual orientation was fixed, there was a potential for fluctuation throughout my life. That relieved me of the need to label myself and act according to the prescriptions of that label. I stopped trying to define who and what I am and tried to simply become more observant and curious. I talk to so many women now who say, "I identify as such-and-such, but it's more complicated than that."

Human sexuality is complex and wonderful. It can also be shocking and disturbing. I've listened to straight friends in a heterosexual marriage confide that they found themselves suddenly and unexpectedly attracted to a friend. Diamond describes this as a connection that "makes it possible to start out with strong platonic (that is, nonsexual) feelings of love for another person, and sometimes develop new and unexpected sexual desires for that person as a result. This occurs because love and desire, despite being separate processes, nonetheless have strong cultural, psychological, and neurobiological links between them."[3] Of course, most close relationships between heterosexual women are simply affectionate without romantic or sexual feelings.

MIXED ORIENTATION MARRIAGES

One of the things I observed that frightened me was that while there were numerous examples of Latter-day Saint mixed-orientation marriages failing, I didn't see the successful ones. As I've come to know more people in the Latter-day Saint/LGBTQ community, I realize there are many quietly successful marriages, which become visible only if they end. This invisibility unfortunately supports the narrative that mixed orientation marriages (MOMs) are doomed to failure; that can be the most dramatic and visible story, but those marriages are not representative of the whole group.

Many of the women I interviewed are or had been married to men. Marriage is a delicate balance of attraction, love, shared goals, hard work, emotional connection, and a multitude of other factors. Same-sex attraction adds an additional component to that mix, and some couples choose to end the marriage in the best interests of one or both partners. I talked to gay women who would have stayed in their traditional marriages but didn't have that option. Other women felt that their MOM marriage was a betrayal of a deep part of them that needed to be free to find fulfillment in a same-sex relationship. Some of us are finding happiness and success in our MOMs. Every woman, whatever her circumstances and choices, was sincere in trying to find the best way forward for her, and they often turned to God for help and guidance.

Both David and I want to stay married to each other, and we have been grateful to see that we are not alone. Other couples like us are also finding happiness and satisfaction in their relationships.

The Four Options Survey gives us a picture of the state of MOMs. It is a research study focused on certain life experiences of Latter-day Saint participants who experience or have experienced same-sex attraction. "Four Options" refers to the four groups of participants the survey studied: 1) single and celibate; 2) single and not celibate; 3) same-sex relationship; and 4) mixed-orientation relationships. The survey studied a variety of factors amongst these groups, including mental health, life and relationship satisfaction, and religion/spirituality. In contrast to the popular narrative that says all mixed-orientation marriages are either doomed to failure or misery, the study found that LGB people in over 500 mixed-orientation marriages surveyed reported that 28% were highly satisfied in their marriage, with 80% overall reporting some level of satisfaction.

Several factors influence satisfaction in a mixed-orientation relationship, including these:

- Meeting needs for connection, intimacy, and mutual understanding
- Expressing sexuality in ways that feel best
- Experiencing more other-sex attraction (heterosexual)
- Resolving issues around depression

- Resolving conflict between faith and sexuality[4]

I look at these factors in terms of what enhances my relationship with my husband and what detracts from it. In the study, authors note the value of encouraging clients to "consider their attraction/aversion to their partner rather than to people generally, as this was found to be more impactful for outcomes in mixed-orientation marriages."[5] In other words, I only need to be attracted to one man: my husband. The fact that in general I am more attracted to women than to men is separate from the distinct relationship that David and I have built together, especially as we have been intentional about strengthening our emotional connection, intimacy, and mutual understanding. Before I met David, I was not interested in marriage. I was focused on school, and I dated, but for fun, not marriage (I was unusual at Ricks College in the 1980s). When I met him, suddenly marriage became a possibility. Could I have fallen in love with and successfully married a different man? I don't know. All I know is I love David, and we are happy.

Most of the women I talked to in mixed-orientation marriages are intentional with their husbands about the way they build and protect their relationship:

- Sarah is grateful for her husband's resolve to stay with her. He is supportive in her finding her own way.
- Jane and her husband put a priority on their shared goals and objectives; she states that neither wants the suffering that comes from going outside the gospel dynamic.
- "Your values—fidelity, trustworthiness, etc.—are independent of your orientation," Daniela says. "You need to take time to talk to each other. Be intentional about communication."
- Erin says they focus on their faith in God. "We have started reading scriptures again together. It's really helped us. We're praying together. We go on walks. Sometimes we bring stuff up. We're open and honest and talk to each other while walking."
- McKell and her husband "start with open communication— how we're feeling, how we're doing. We're not out to get each

other. We love each other; we trust each other. We depend on communication, trust, talking about feelings."

- Jane describes their relationship as including "play, talk, a lot of reading, exercise, family home evening, prayer, and scripture study." It's beneficial when she validates his opinion; she sees he values that, so she's willing to stop what she's doing and talk even at inconvenient times.

- Wally describes working with her husband to decide "do we truly want each other, are we happy and satisfied?" She says they depend on openness and honesty, being proactive in their relationship rather than reactive.

These marriages depend on communication and intentional strengthening of their love and trust for each other. All marriages will benefit from the same commitment to connection and goals they described, but the impact of the SSA dynamic in the relationship requires even more intentional communication and honesty.

I opened up to David eight years ago, and after those early discussions, we didn't say much about my attraction to women for four or five years. I worried that he didn't want to talk about it. I didn't know what more to say, or even if it was something we would ever talk about again. I think we needed time to sit with that truth. David needed time to see my intent. As our relationship grew stronger and I became braver and healthier, the Spirit worked on both of us to move forward, and we were prepared to integrate this part of my life experience and grow together. A few months ago, in a letter to our children when we told them about my increasing public openness, David described our intention:

> We promised each other when we were married that we would be faithful to each other, and we have been, and we are. We also promised that we would give everything we are and possess to the building of God's kingdom. The kingdom of God is not chapels and temples; it is his children.
>
> Whatever the feelings you currently have for the Church, the reason your parents are still married is because of our faith in God and our belief in His Church. . . . We hope that the love you experienced in our home and the challenges we all faced together will be a foundation of strength and pattern for success for you as you wrestle with your own problems. . . .

So rest assured, Meghan and I are walking side-by-side. I had no real idea when we married what a magnificent partner had joined her future to mine. We are individuals and yet so much more together. We have different gifts and different challenges. We serve at home and at Church in different capacities, but the commitment we have made is to serve together as best as we know how. I hope you can learn to respect and appreciate our choices [including greater openness].

It is an act of faith for both of us to write and speak about my sexual orientation, our lessons learned, our marriage, and how we are making our way forward one day at a time. It takes effort and humility to talk to each other about what we are feeling and what we need. It's not a smooth, paved road we're on, but we have always preferred the trail through the woods that is less traveled.

Notes for Chapter Seven

1   Lisa M. Diamond, *Sexual Fluidity: Understanding Women's Love and Desire* (Cambridge, MA: Harvard University Press, 2009), 210.

2   Ibid, 184.

3   Ibid, 203.

4   "Purpose of the Survey: PowerPoint of Findings," (n.d.), http://4optionssurvey.com/. Retrieved March 26, 2021.

5   Bridges, J. G., Lefevor, G. T., & Schow, R. L, *Sexual Satisfaction and Mental Health in Mixed-Orientation Relationships: A Mormon Sample of Sexual Minority Partners* (2019), http://4optionssurvey.com/wp-content/uploads/2020/08/Mormons-in-MORs.pdf. Retrieved March 26, 2021.

Chapter Eight

SHEDDING SHAME TO
BEGIN HEALING

Four years after I told David I was attracted to women, I sat at lunch with my dear friend Jen. I had confided in her soon after that first conversation with David, and she had been the ideal of empathy, compassion, and wisdom from day one. Interestingly, she had earlier been prompted by the Spirit to know what was troubling me. I wonder if the Lord prepared some of my friends in advance, so they would be able to process their own feelings and be ready to be present and compassionate when I did open up to them.

During those first years following my discussion with David about my attraction to women, we returned to a status quo. Real growth in our relationship was still in the future. I didn't see a benefit in talking about it further. I continued to feel broken, but I didn't know what to do in response to those feelings. I didn't slip back into full-blown denial, but certainly into dismissiveness with a heavy coating of shame. I clung to the Atonement of Jesus Christ and hoped He would give me further light and knowledge at some point.

The four years since talking to David had been not just a roller-coaster but a ride on the Wild Mouse, filled with unexpected turns at a terrifying speed. I seemed to lurch from one depressive episode to the next, managing to teach my institute class and show up to help my daughters with new grandbabies but never knowing what emotional/mental state was coming next. My friends had probably taken the worst of it as I careened between needing them and coldly withdrawing from them. I had begun to worry about making commitments that were a few months out because I didn't know what my mental state would be at any given point. Jen had a front row seat to all of it. As we ate lunch together, I told Jen I'd had the impression I should pray to be healed from depression and its attendant instability.

Depression isn't an easy fix. It can take medication and therapy (and luck in both) to make any progress. Years before, I had accepted that I had a recurrent mental disorder that would be part of my experience in mortality. Never had I considered simply asking God to take it away. But the impression kept growing, and I decided to ask. It felt like an inspired question and an inspired prayer.

In retrospect, I believe that prayer was exercising my agency to initiate a painful growth process that would change my life. God didn't force the change on me, but He invited me to take a step forward if I wished. Eventually, that growth process began to relieve me of the shame-induced depression I had battled for most of my adult life.

TAKING A CHANCE ON LIGHT AND TRUTH

The first hard step forward began when I came across Brené Brown's work, which helped me to recognize the destructive power of shame in my life. She writes:

> If you put shame in a petri dish and cover it with judgment, silence, and secrecy, it grows out of control until it consumes everything in sight—you have basically provided shame with the environment it needs to thrive. On the other hand, if you put shame in a petri dish and douse it with empathy, shame loses power and starts to fade. Empathy creates a hostile environment for shame—it can't survive.[1]

I later heard her say in an interview that the antidote for shame is to speak our truth and be met with empathy and compassion.

Those words kept reverberating in my mind. *The antidote to shame is to speak my truth.* That is the very thing I avoided with all the energy of mind and heart in my life up to that point, but I felt the Spirit telling me to speak. I recoiled in fear, yet my desire to be free from the damaging effects of shame was so great that I finally resolved to try truth. In Twelve Step programs there is a slogan that says when the pain of the problem is greater than the pain of the solution, we are ready to act. I was ready to act.

I prayed to know who would receive my truth with empathy and compassion. I knew that was an essential part of the shame antidote. I had to talk to the right people. I felt impressed to talk to a friend who had a gift of being fully present; I felt truly seen and heard by her in the past, and I knew she would respond with compassion.

The other person I felt guided to open up to was a good friend who happened to be our stake president. I didn't need to talk to him as a priesthood leader receiving a confession. I was not looking for help to repent because I hadn't sinned (and I clarified that with him up front). I wanted him to see me and help me hold this truth about myself, and I trusted his compassion and empathy.

I arranged to meet separately with each of these friends in private settings, face to face. Those first discussions were so hard. My heart raced, and I felt nausea and shortness of breath. I didn't feel an immediate relief from the shame, but as I left the stake president's office, he looked intently at me and thanked me for my service to the women in the stake. Then he told me I was good, and he trusted me. It was something I had heard many times before, but for the first time I didn't hear the voice saying, *He doesn't know me. If he really knew me, he wouldn't say that.* The deceptive voice was silenced because I *was* seen and still found worthy of love, acceptance, and trust. He saw the real, whole Meghan, and I could finally allow myself to believe the truth of what he said.

A week or so later, I was at lunch with another close friend, and I started to feel the nudge to tell her. That feeling is similar to an urgent invitation to bear testimony on Fast Sunday, but it is much less welcome. The feelings of nausea and anxiety began, and I pushed the food around on my plate for some time before I asked if I could share something with her. After a few moments of taking in what I was saying to her and assimilating it with what she already knew about me, she recovered and said, "I think I love you more now than ever." She told me later that she was amazed at my vulnerability in an effort to be authentic. Being seen and loved was an incredible feeling composed of fear, freedom, honesty, and an acceptance that I could believe and embrace. Shame is a huge barrier to connection with others; coming out of silence and secrecy allowed me to also come out of hiding and into the warmth of true community.

In the Book of Mormon, Jacob teaches that "the Spirit speaketh the truth and lieth not. Wherefore, it speaketh of things as they really are, and of things as they really will be" (Jacob 4:13). When I was able to clear away the clutter of shame that interfered with the Spirit, I could receive and believe truths about myself, about who I really am, and about who I can become. The voice of the accuser was muted and the Spirit's influence amplified, giving me hope and an ability to believe in God's love and acceptance of me. Elder Rasband explains how the love of God clears out obstacles that interfere with hearing the Spirit: "There is no room for fear in these holy places of God or in the hearts of His children. Why? Because of love. God loves us— always—and we love Him. Our love of God counters all fears, and His love abounds in holy places."[2]

It is only in retrospect that I now recognize my episodes of depression coincided with waves of attraction to women, or a specific woman, and shame accompanied those feelings. I can observe the connection between a time of intense but buried attraction to someone and a major depressive episode. *It was not my attraction to women that caused me to spiral into depression; it was the shame I attached to those feelings.* I feel great compassion as I look back on my younger, suffering self.

I'm currently participating in a group for Latter-day Saint women who experience attraction to women or gender dysphoria. The experience of suicidal depression as a result of attraction to a friend, roommate, or mission companion while in denial and hiding is shared by everyone in the group. Silence, secrecy, and self-judgment are countered by speaking the truth and being met with empathy and compassion. That is the antidote for shame's poison.

As Rebecca said, "God wants me to love this aspect of myself, and shame makes that hard." Her fear of rejection from her church community and family is poignant, but she feels an absolute decrease in shame from talking with others. Her end goal is to be totally open, publicly out. She feels shame return when she has to censor herself. She has come to believe the risk of rejection is worth the reward of self-acceptance.

Linda was in denial, as I was, for decades. She lived a long time feeling she was irreparably broken in some way. Admitting her same-sex attraction was not her idea, she says, it was in response to an invitation and prompting from God to come out of denial. When the world slowed down during the COVID restrictions, she said, "I had to stop running. I had to spend a lot of time in self-reflection, study by myself for church, and pause to pray and listen to the Spirit." She added podcasts to her scripture study, and she came across one by Becky and Bennet Borden.[3] As she listened, the Spirit reinforced Becky's message, saying to her "Linda, you're not broken, you're just gay. And I love you." That message felt truthful and right to her, and over the next few days she realized it was the missing puzzle piece that put everything together. She felt relief as the incongruencies in her life resolved.

Natasha shares a similar experience of self-acceptance and peace. She had always been fun and free-spirited until she got married and tried to fit the roles she thought were expected of her. Discovering that she is gay helped her feel like she was coming back to herself. She was able to say, "That is me, I'm finally myself again. I make sense now." As she is more honest with herself, she says, "Every area of our marriage is improving; our sex life is way better because being vulnerable is such a huge part of sexuality. I am attracted to him, and his attraction for me has improved, as who I am has become a part of our life. I honestly don't think either of us would change anything about our relationship."

David has compared observing my changes over the last year to watching a tightly closed bud open and bloom. Now that I am no longer hiding, I can be more confident and comfortable in my own skin.

SHAME DISSIPATES IN LIGHT

Shame still flares up for me from time to time, almost exclusively when I feel I am hiding. I know there are people who wonder why I have to talk about this at all. It is uncomfortable and distasteful to them, but I don't do it for them. I am opening up because when I start to slip back into the shadows to hide, it is poison to me. That doesn't mean I wave a pride flag everywhere I go (though I do wear a rainbow pin, to let others know I am a safe person for them). It means that if I silence myself at a time when I would otherwise comment, I am hiding. It was frustrating when I would testify to my classes of feeling the power of the Atonement in times of great need because I felt I had to be vague about the circumstances. If it had been our house burning down or a cancer diagnosis, I would naturally speak of it. But because my path to the Savior's arms passed through same-sex attraction, I would only talk in general terms, hiding who I am and my greatest spiritual experiences with the power of God's love and comfort. And even as I bore a general testimony of divine love and power, I felt shame as I hid myself once more.

I found relief from that shame even if there was only one person in my Gospel Doctrine class who knew I was bisexual (how I described myself initially). As I bore my testimony at the end of class, I knew that one person was seeing me fully, and that was enough. I didn't have to broadcast to the whole class; it would have distracted from my purpose at the time, which was to testify of Christ, not do a big reveal. But those few friends seeing me took away my feeling of hiding and unworthiness until I became ready to open up to more people.

One of the most important of those discussions happened with my daughter, Mary Beth. I was talking to her on the phone, and we were discussing her moving in with a new roommate, when she surprised herself by telling me they weren't just friends; they were dating. She was crying and afraid of my disappointment or—even worse—rejection. My reassurances seemed to fall short until I finally told her that I was also attracted to women, and I had been since I was a teenager. We both cried together as we reached a new level of honesty with each other. When I heard her finally believe that I would not reject her and that I really did understand, I thought, "If this is the only reason for my same-sex attraction, it's worth it." Coming out to each other was a big step for us and a step toward my own self-acceptance.

I've learned to sit with my feelings in the space between cravings and aversion, without either getting lost in the craving or running away in aversion. This helps me to be teachable without self-judgment. Now when I feel a wave of attraction to women, rather than burying it under shame, I can be curious about what's going on. Am I feeling a lack of connection in my key relationships? Am I feeling fear and yearning for comfort? How can I honor that need for a deeper connection to women in a way that also supports my relationship with David and God?

This curiosity helps me to learn and grow rather than wallow in self-judgment. If I am simply feeling drawn to a strong, smart, beautiful woman, I allow myself to pursue a friendship. We probably have a lot in common and will enjoy talking to each other and spending time together. When I run away from it, the attraction gains power, but when I lean into getting to know that woman, the person becomes whole to me, another daughter of God, not an object of my entitlement. If I don't beat myself up for noticing someone, I am able to respond from a healthier place. A wonderful effect of this is that as I am gentler with myself, I become less judgmental of others.

Shame cannot exist in the light of acceptance and love. When I asked God to relieve me of depression, I didn't understand what it would require of me. But because I acted on that spiritual nudge to speak my truth, I began to be healed in ways I could not anticipate. I didn't know how powerfully shame triggered my predisposition to depression or that the removal of that trigger would start me on a healing path spiritually, emotionally, and physically. Shame almost killed me. Honesty, empathy and compassion helped to heal me.

Notes for Chapter Eight

1   Brené Brown, *Gifts of Imperfection*, (Center City, MN: Hazelden Publishing, 2010).

2   Ronald A. Rasband, "Be Not Troubled." *Ensign,* November 2018.

3   Becky and Bennet Borden, "Real Talk with Ganel-Lun Condie and Scott Sorensen," *Come Follow Me: Real Talk*, podcast, https://www.youtube.com/watch?v=N7czPEpox9w.

Chapter Nine

CHALLENGES AND CHOICES

After talking to my three friends about my attraction to women, I didn't feel a need to tell anyone else. I had trusted friends in the classes I taught, so I felt seen. In addition, my stake president knew that I was serving in stake callings as a closeted gay woman, and I felt accepted and trusted by him. I was in a good place. Unfortunately, my contentment would only last a couple of weeks. I decided to tell one more person. We had become friends in a community group, and I was supporting her through a difficult time. We were close, and I didn't want her to be blindsided if she heard this information about me from others.

I was the one who was blindsided; she responded the next day with an expression of romantic attraction toward me. It shattered the balance I thought I had achieved. She had never felt attraction toward another woman, and it was shocking for her too. I had not thought of her in a context other than friendship, but when she started to talk to me about what she had been feeling, I instantly felt a strong similar attraction toward her. I already cared about her deeply as a friend, and a switch flipped to add in romantic feelings. Suddenly, the hypothetical and fearful question "What would I do if I ever developed feelings for someone who felt the same way?" became frighteningly real. I had avoided this possibility all my life by keeping myself hidden and protected. I saw myself as an overweight grandma and assumed no one would ever be attracted to me. These sudden romantic feelings for my friend blew their way past my lame external boundaries of secrecy and negative body image. Mutual attraction had always been a far-fetched scenario, so I didn't have internal boundaries created. This was a totally new experience. I wasn't ready.

Nothing ever happened between my friend and me that violated covenants. She respected my values, and she was also committed to integrity in her marriage. Even so, the "I know we can't do this, but I wish we could" atmosphere crushed my undeveloped internal boundaries. I had talked and taught about resisting temptation, but I still didn't know enough. I mistook a candle flame for temptation, and I was unprepared when it became a raging wildfire stealing oxygen from the air.

I talked to my husband almost immediately, because I needed external support and safety. I also talked to my stake president, the one who just weeks before told me he trusted me completely. I felt that the floor had opened up under my feet and was ready to swallow me whole. Did I imagine I knew what this would feel like? I was not even close.

My stake president listened to me, and his response surprised me. He said he didn't think I needed to end the friendship—I should just set some boundaries, like emailing instead of texting because texting was too impulsive and immediate. He also, with some hesitancy, told me he was surprised by what he was going to say next, but he had a strong impression that he should ask me to refrain from taking the sacrament for two weeks. He emphasized this request was not a punishment but an unexpected prompting from the Spirit.

My husband gave me a blessing, and in it he told me to establish boundaries but not to cut off the friendship. I was shocked. Why were both of these men, acting under inspiration, telling me to stay put? Wasn't I supposed to run in the other direction?

I reached out to a woman I had talked to previously after watching her *Voices of Hope*[1] video—she advised me to get a Latter-day Saint therapist experienced in SSA work, and she offered to make a call to one she knew. He ended up being a perfect fit. I decided that if he told me to cut off contact with my friend, I would do it, regardless of what anyone else said. It just didn't make sense to me to stay connected to someone when the relationship felt so dangerous.

LEARNING HAPPENS IN RELATIONSHIPS

In the initial meeting with my new therapist, Mark[2], my first question was about whether I should end the friendship. His response surprised me: "Learning happens in relationships." He went on to say, *"Staying in this relationship would be a powerful exercise in the development of internal and interpersonal boundaries."* When he said that, I felt a powerful jolt of confirmation from the Spirit. He compared staying in the friendship to spelunking into a cave: with the appropriate anchors and safety measures, we can explore what otherwise would be too dangerous. Mark told me my openness with a supportive network of people—my husband, my stake president, a close friend, and my therapist—as well as my friend's respect for my values, provided safety anchors that could make it possible to stay in the relationship and learn in it.

This was so unexpected that it took confirmation from God for me to let go of my expectations and trust the Lord and my advisors. I began to get practice in setting and maintaining internal and interpersonal boundaries.

In retrospect, I can see that I had boundary problems and a codependent relationship with my friend long before I talked to her about my attraction to women. As she had described painful experiences with her husband, I began to feel protective of her. I now see this as a dangerous boundary failure for me. When I start to feel protective of a woman, it is an open door that can lead to romantic feelings. I have learned a lot about how to maintain healthy relationships from looking back on my boundary fails.

My two-week restriction from taking the sacrament also gave me clarifying insight into what my covenant relationship with God means to me. I was a week into it before I realized I couldn't go to the temple. Two weeks of thinking about what was most important to me was a critical part of my early boundary work. I felt a profound sense of loss at my temporary exclusion from those covenants, and I saw clearly what was at stake in my choices. That temporary restriction helped me strengthen my commitment to improving my infant boundaries. Today, years later, I express gratitude every Saturday night that I will be able to receive the sacrament the following day.

The intensity of the romantic feelings I experienced toward my friend surprised me. In high school, years earlier, I had received a couple of invitations to become romantically involved with friends. I considered and rejected the offers because I knew I would be repenting a few days later, and that seemed so dishonest. I see now that the choice was easy because I simply wasn't physically attracted to either girl. The women I *was* attracted to as a teenager or adult were secret crushes, so my "secrecy boundary" provided protection. But now it was an entirely new experience, where friendship, attraction, and reciprocity finally aligned.

I eventually realized that the power of my feelings was not as much based on a specific person as on my finally experiencing the unstifled power of my attraction to women. I had not felt a romantic attraction to my friend until after she expressed feelings for me, and then I was astonished at the intensity of my response. She was the first person I was attracted to after I accepted my orientation and began to open up to others. Without the bunker of shame burying my feelings, they hit me with an unexpected power.

In retrospect, I recognize it was probably a manifestation of "gay puberty," a delayed reaction in adults who are accepting their same-sex attraction for the first time. This reaction mimics the biological and social process of adolescence, and when it has been suppressed can manifest itself later in life.

Roberta describes a similar experience. She came out to herself and a friend on a weekend, and the next day at work suddenly found her co-worker "the most attractive woman in world." As Roberta finally acknowledged her attraction to women, those feelings strengthened to the point that she was distracted by almost any woman. This intensity lasted for 4 to 5 months, as her sexual feelings transitioned from the power of a burst dam, releasing everything that had been held behind it, to a steady and manageable stream. During that time, she focused on determining her boundaries and figuring out the role shame and guilt played in her life.

I, too, was entering a new growth phase of learning about and creating boundaries that would enable me to drop my immature and inadequate boundary of denial and move into a more honest and self-accepting approach to my life.

LEARNING FROM OUR OWN EXPERIENCE

My experience is not unique—a close friendship suddenly shifting from the affectional domain to the romantic. Women who have never experienced attraction to other women find themselves constantly thinking about a friend at church, a neighbor, or co-worker who is emotionally available and caring. This aspect of sexual fluidity can be terrifying to the temple-attending, married-with-kids, casseroles-for-new-moms woman who wonders what meaning it has for her. What has she been hiding from herself? Is she flawed in some way that will keep her from eternity with her family? She may feel deep regret—often for years and years—for the thoughts and feelings that seemingly ambushed her.

Sophie[3] is a mom with young children and a husband who is busy with work and church. She is emotionally starved. Her friendship with another member of the Relief Society presidency provides what she is missing in her marriage relationship—she feels seen and heard and valued. When she is with her friend, she feels alive, and when they are apart, she longs for the next time they will be together. She feels grateful that God sent her this dear friend. She longs for the friendship's depth of emotional connection in her sexual expression with her husband, and she begins to imagine what it would be like to be with her friend in that intimate way. The joy she feels in her friendship shifts into shame and fear. She wonders what is wrong with her, and she becomes unwilling to pray because she thinks God must be disappointed in her. She wonders if she is living an inauthentic life as a woman married to a man and what that means for her future and her family.

When Sophie begins to understand that her feelings for her friend are a normal expression of human sexuality, she becomes less fearful and ashamed. She is able to accept her own sexual fluidity, realizing that it doesn't force her into any future she doesn't desire for herself. If she wants to stay committed to her family, she can observe the pull of her attraction to her friend and decide how she wants to respond to that in a way that protects her most important relationships. She might decide to set internal and external boundaries for herself, and she may talk to her husband about her need for deeper emotional connection with him.

Sophie might instead realize that she wants an intimate relationship with her friend, especially if she finds those romantic feelings are mutual. As a member of the Church, she is then faced with a decision about how and whether to respond to that desire in a way that is congruent with her values, goals, commitments and, ultimately, what she really wants for her future.

The determining factor for Sophie is that she gets to decide. She decides what she wants. She decides how she will respond. If she feels a strong desire for a woman, she has the option of determining what to do in response to that desire. Romantic attraction is not defining. It offers a choice, and each option brings with it consequences. Deciding which of the consequences to live with is an essential part of the decision-making process.

For me, and the majority of the women I talked to, wrestling with these options in prayer is critical.

Throughout my life, I had resisted pursuing my attraction to women. But when I was faced with a woman who was also attracted to me, suddenly the game changed. I was facing my biggest fear, and that moved me out of hypothetical "what if this ever happens" and into reality.

One of the first lessons I quickly learned was "If it's not tempting, it's not a temptation." All those stories I heard growing up about saying no to a cigarette or a beer paled in comparison to what I was feeling. This was like a huge ocean wave hitting me, hurling me off my feet and tossing and turning me with its immense power. At one point I said to a friend that the temptation felt overwhelming, and they said, "It's not. Because you weren't overwhelmed." That's true, but only barely. The urge to step outside my integrity, to act against my deepest-held values, to hurt the people I love the most was incredibly powerful. And I had so many points of safety that many other women don't have: a kind and emotionally-available husband, a compassionate stake president, and an insightful and supportive therapist. This awareness of my own vulnerability completely wiped out my judgment of others who make a different choice than I did. The pull is real and powerful.

During this time, I was teaching a class on the Atonement of Jesus Christ. The Savior's experience in Gethsemane resonated with me. It was real. His cry for the cup to be removed was not theater, according to Elder Neal A. Maxwell. The Savior's experience was *almost* overwhelming. Elder Maxwell says:

> In Gethsemane, the suffering Jesus began to be "sore amazed" (Mark 14:33), or, in the Greek, "awestruck" and "astonished."
>
> Imagine, Jehovah, the Creator of this and other worlds, "astonished!" Jesus knew cognitively what He must do, but not experientially. He had never personally known the exquisite and exacting process of an atonement before. Thus, when the agony came in its fulness, it was so much, much worse than even He with his unique intellect had ever imagined! No wonder an angel appeared to strengthen him! (See Luke 22:43.)[4]

Heavenly Father didn't send us to mortality to go through the motions of temptation. It has to be real, just as it was for the Savior in Gethsemane. I realized that rather than feeling weak and guilty for my desires, I could recognize in them the purposes of mortality at work and the invitation to discern my real needs, those deepest desires of my heart that ultimately motivate my choices and actions. I also find in Elder Maxwell's words reassurance that the Savior understands. He understands the agony that can drive us into choices we may come to regret, and He has so much compassion and empathy for us in those moments.

As I became less judgmental of others, my mind expanded to accept that the Lord may not view my struggles with a readiness to condemn me but rather to understand and sit with me and empathize with me in my pain.

That patient compassion is as true for Sophie, who experienced one episode of attraction for a friend, as it is for gay and bisexual women who may fall in love with friends time and time again throughout their lives. We choose how to respond to each experience of our lives, and our Savior is always regarding us with tender love and compassion.

CHOOSING TO SET BOUNDS

I loved hearing the answers to my interview question about boundaries. It was an opportunity for me to learn from women who are wiser and more experienced than me, and I picked up a lot of great tips! I still tend toward secrecy and shame if I am feeling a magnetic pull toward someone, but I learned from these women that honesty and bringing feelings into the light is essential.

Boundaries can be challenged by a profound desire for the emotionally-connected physical relationship women may feel is lacking in their lives. Sarah says she feels somewhat emotionally connected in her marriage but confides, "the level of emotional connection I can achieve with women, my husband can never and will never get to. If there was a unicorn of a man that could do that, he'd probably be gay anyway." When she fell in love with her best friend, the whole earth moved beneath her feet. "With my friend, I would never go there, though that feels really tragic. It is so excruciatingly painful to want something you can never have, in this case romance and intimacy. I just don't get to experience those feelings safely."

Wendy describes a process of boundary building as a result of mistakes made during her own gay puberty, when she felt entitled to everything that was taken from her. She felt she had every right to know what it felt like to kiss a woman and be intimate and experience someone feeling the same affection for her. She said, "I would justify it by saying I was just looking for healthy physical touch. When I did cross a line, I saw the hurt that it caused, the pain to my husband and the other women involved. I moved into Twelve Steps, and that has saved my life. Now I can see the past codependent cycles in relationships. I can look at my own behavior and take responsibility for my anger, grief, and resentment. I am learning how to be loving and kind and affirming to myself."

Elizabeth explains how her boundaries are context-specific: she has a close gay friend that she can camp with because she doesn't have romantic feelings for her. On the other hand, it is too difficult to even ride in a car with another friend for whom she feels strong attraction.

Jane's early boundary was "I would rather live with longing than guilt." When she fell in love with a friend, she realized that her feelings were strong, but if the gospel were true, she could be harming someone's potential to be with God. Later, feeling that she needed to act on her desires in order to feel better, she asked in prayer, "Is it okay I'm gay?" Her answer was "Yes, it's okay. I have a plan for you; hang on." She chose to trust God and wait. She now knows that God doesn't hate her because of how she feels but that He is giving her personalized experiences that will help her become fully developed. She recognizes that "disappointment can live with joy, and mercy and justice working together create a great power." Her boundaries have matured to include self-acceptance, honesty with her husband and friends, and talking to her husband when she feels a magnetic pull toward a woman, so the attraction can lose its power.

Leila Jane talks with her husband about crushes she has. They are usually women who are very queer and confident. She leans into relationships where there is a spark. She wants to explore that attraction, not sexually, but recognizing that her body and soul want to connect. She is not afraid of that desire for connection, because she is grounded in herself and her intention for her marriage. Being able to talk with her husband about her crushes and attractions has strengthened her marriage.

I learned that secrecy and my negative body image had been my weak and passive boundaries in the past. Moving forward, especially as I acknowledged my same-sex attraction and the fact that women might be attracted to me, I needed something better. I wanted to be grounded in my own values and internal boundaries, and I had to decide for myself what that would look like.

Alma declares that God "granted unto men according to their desires" (Alma 29:4). Lehi teaches of the benefit of facing opposition—contrasting and compelling choices—so that we can exercise agency and act for ourselves, rather than being acted upon. He tells us we could not act for ourselves, "save it should be that [we are] enticed by the one or the other" (2 Nephi 2:16). The deepest desires of my heart were not clear to me until my various desires collided with each other, and I had to choose. In that choice I found what defined me.

Elder Maxwell teaches, "what we insistently desire, over time, is what we will eventually become and what we will receive in the eternity."[5] I don't believe that is a threat but simply descriptive of the

Lord's love and mercy for us. We receive according to the desires of our hearts. We think that everyone will want to be in the highest degree of the celestial kingdom and become a god. But godhood is a tough, selfless job that makes mothering demanding and unappreciative toddlers look like a breeze. I wonder if that will be the desire of everyone's heart.

In Doctrine and Covenants section 7, the Lord is addressing Peter's feelings about John's request to stay on the earth until the Lords' return. Did Peter feel jealous or ashamed because he didn't think of that request first? Whatever the cause, Jesus says to Peter:

> If I will that he tarry till I come, what is that to thee? For he desired of me that he might bring souls unto me, but thou desiredst that thou might speedily come unto me in my kingdom.
>
> Verily I say unto you, ye shall both have according to your desires, for ye both joy in that which ye have desired.

While the Lord asks me to surrender my will to His, He also honors the desires of my heart. Through the experiences I had that challenged my decision to marry and honor my covenants, I discerned their value. I went deep into my soul and discovered those covenants matter profoundly to me—I love the Savior, and my covenants with Him cement my most important relationship. David gets to choose too, and he has chosen to stay with me. As my husband and I deepen our love and trust for each other, we strengthen our decision to choose each other. The desire of my heart is for a path forward that will protect my relationship with God and with David.

Other women have different desires, and different circumstances and options, and so they may make different choices. As I listen to women's stories, I wonder to myself "How would my life be different if I had been in her situation? What choices would I have made?" I believe I would have always come back to God and my covenants, but the road may have been more circuitous. I see how ridiculous it is for me to judge anyone else's life. I am grateful that the Savior is aware of all the factors influencing our decisions, that He has felt everything we feel, and that He always works in our lives for good.

We are revealed to ourselves through the choices we make. Those choices may change over time, as we grow into a truer version of ourselves. I've quoted Lehi and Alma—now it's time for Yogi Berra: "It ain't over till it's over." I worried that any misstep would have eternal consequences, and I had to get it right the first time. But the purpose of earth life is growth, and growth often comes through learning from our mistakes. Because of the Savior's Atonement, when we turn to Him, there is no failure, only growth. That doesn't mean there are no consequences; if I had an affair with my friend, would my marriage have survived? Would my children have forgiven me? I don't know the answer to those questions, though I have seen them play out in other lives, with various outcomes. But I do know that "Repentance is not the back-up plan, it is the plan," as Elder Neil A. Andersen says.[6]

I can learn from my experiences without being condemned for them. I often make mistakes that hurt myself and others. Fortunately, the game doesn't get called in the middle for a player's error. We play all the way to the end, with the Lord involved the whole way. He is intent on our growth, and all our experiences work together toward that end as we learn to know ourselves.

Notes for Chapter Nine

1   I watched a lot of *Voices of Hope* videos; they are personal stories of queer members of the church, created and hosted by North Star, a faith-affirming resource for LGBTQ Latter-day Saints who want to keep their behavior aligned with Church teachings. You can find these stories at www.northstarlds.org/voices-of-hope/.

2   I use a pseudonym for my therapist since you are reading my interpretation and memories of his work rather than his own words.

3   Unlike the other individual women I quote, "Sophie" is a composite of many women with the same story.

4   Neal A. Maxwell, "Willing to Submit," *Ensign*, May 1985.

5   Neal A. Maxwell, "According to the Desires of Our Hearts," *Ensign*, November 1996.

6   Neil A. Andersen, "Teaching Repentance: The Powerful Combination of the Scriptures and *Preach My Gospel*," 2018 Mission Leadership Seminar, June 25, 2018.

Chapter Ten

HEALING HAPPENS IN RELATIONSHIPS

I was surprised by my husband's and stake president's counsel to stay in a relationship with my friend while forming healthy boundaries. I kept thinking about the analogy that tells us to drive as far away from the edge of the cliff as possible and the scriptural warnings to avoid the very appearance of evil. Mark, my therapist, had advised me that I could learn and grow through this friendship. But shouldn't I play it safe with my eternal salvation and my family's happiness? Even as I felt the truth of what he said, it seemed to contradict years of lessons, talks, and my own expectations.

This was not the first time that inspired counsel from others and directly from God would explode my expectations. Eventually I came to understand that playing it safe was not staying away from any possibility of temptation; safety is found in facing challenges in the strength of the Lord. Elder Dieter F. Uchtdorf explains this beautifully:

> Would you honestly want everything spelled out in every detail? Would you honestly want every question answered? Every destination mapped out?
>
> I believe most of us would tire very quickly of this sort of heavenly micromanagement. We learn the important lessons of life through experience. Through learning from our mistakes. Through repenting and realizing for ourselves that "wickedness never was happiness."

Jesus Christ, the Son of God, died so that our mistakes might not condemn us and forever halt our progress. Because of Him, we can repent, and our mistakes can become stepping-stones to greater glory."[1]

The week following my unexpected situation with my friend, we left for a family vacation. We were meeting all of our children and their families at the Outer Banks of North Carolina. We rented a house for a week, and we planned on days at the beach, pool parties, great food, and good times together. The week prior, I had been joyously looking forward to time with my family. By the time we gathered, I was weighed down with shame, fear, and confusion. I was unable to take the sacrament with my family, though no one happened to notice. But I watched my grandchildren gather around the bread tray and realized I couldn't participate in this covenant that day, and that reality was crushing. I was a mess, and I couldn't hide it.

One evening I was sitting in the backyard, dangling my feet in the water, looking at the bottom of the pool, and wishing I was there. My youngest daughter sneaked up behind me and poured a cup of ice water over me. Everyone expected me to jump up, grab her, and throw her in the pool, then start a water fight with the family. That was the mom they knew. This sad woman who simply stood up and walked into the house was a stranger.

After three or four days, I knew I had to talk to them. They were aware something was horribly wrong, and not knowing was worse than the truth. At least, that's what I told myself. I asked four of my five daughters if we could go into my bedroom and talk. Mary Beth was arriving with her girlfriend Julie the next day. We were meeting Julie for the first time that week, and I didn't want to damage her introduction to the family by postponing this discussion any longer. Mary Beth already knew about my same-sex attraction from our coming out to each other earlier in the year.

There is so much I wish I could change about that night. I was sitting on the floor, pressed into a corner, and wishing I could push my way through the wall behind me. I don't remember much of what I said, just that I felt so ashamed and regretful. I knew I was hurting them, and I had tried so hard to protect them from pain.

I told them I experience same-sex attraction. I also told them I had gotten involved with a friend—nothing that broke covenants, but I was not able to take the sacrament for a few weeks. I started out by reassuring them I was staying in the Church and my marriage and family. Even with that reassurance, some of them felt instant fear that I would leave because that was what they observed with friends who came out as gay. Their mom, their super-orthodox mom, their seminary-teacher mom, couldn't take the sacrament. And because I was sure that I couldn't go through this more than once, I was talking to them as a group, not individually. I couldn't bear to have David there too, so they didn't see us united, and my assurances were challenged by the visual impact of seeing me alone without David at my side. It was a room full of shock and hurt and fear and betrayal. I couldn't respond to their need for comfort. All I could do was press myself harder into the wall and wish my existence could just come to an end.

Even now, I find myself shaking as I think about that night. I wish I had been in a more emotionally-healthy place when I told them, so I could have offered more support. But would I have ever told them if I had not literally been pushed to the wall? I don't know. I was afraid then of damage and destruction. I was in the worst nightmare of my life, but I know now it was an important part of the growth of our relationships, tearing down walls and bringing in truth and light.

That was the beginning of more conversations, gradually, over the next few years. It's been a rocky road but an essential one for us to travel. I did have more chances to talk when I was calm. We started building a new kind of trust, one based more in authenticity and grace. One positive outcome is that my kids are less worried about me judging them! This process has taught me to trust in the Lord to give us beauty for ashes.

As Mae told me in our interview, "Sometimes growth feels like digging a grave, but it is actually digging a foundation that's solid and authentic and real."

BECOMING WHOLE AND SEPARATE

Three weeks after that trip to North Carolina, I left home again to go help one of my daughters who had just been diagnosed with breast cancer. I spent several weeks in New York City with her young family as she started chemotherapy. My fear for my daughter was combined with my fear for me, my marriage, and my family. I became desperately open to learning, and the long-distance work I did with my therapist completely shifted my paradigm around my myself. It was frightening yet hopeful at the same time.

One of the first questions my therapist, Mark, asked me regarding my attraction to women was "Do you think this is a bad thing?" That question floored me—how could it not be a bad thing? Isn't it in direct opposition to the plan of salvation? Doesn't it threaten my covenants? If I acted on my feelings, I would destroy my family, lose my membership in the Church, and generally ruin my life. I didn't see good in any of that. His next question invited me to examine that binary, fear-filled framework. He asked, "Why do you assume God wants you to give up your same-sex attraction completely?" Educating our desires, he said, is the way to make them safe. This happens by moving away from fusion with others and into differentiation of self, which requires identity development and the ability to be a healthy and whole self in relation to others. I recognized my need for differentiation in all relationships, not just where I felt a romantic attraction. How often had I merged with the problems of a sister I visit taught? What about the way my mood instantly shifted from happy to ashamed when my kids were critical of me? I decided to work on becoming a separate and whole individual who might respond to others but not merge with them. I also needed to learn how to educate and strengthen my feeble boundaries.

Resisting the impulse to merge or lose myself in others' emotions and needs was critical to healing within this friendship that was suddenly threatening. Staying in the relationship gave me an opportunity to learn from a safe zone. I continued to talk with my husband, close friends, stake president, and therapist. I was honest with all of these people as I worked within the friendship to learn how to create boundaries and recognize what was safe and what was not. My over-arching boundaries were "protect myself," "protect my relationship with David," and "protect my relationship with God." I found that communicating too often or too late at night pushed those boundaries. I decided that for a while I felt more comfortable being in a group together rather than being alone with this friend.

As I've talked with other gay women, I see a consistent self-honesty that enables them to create limits to keep their relationships within the bounds they set for themselves. Wendy says, "Boundaries are healthy. Boundary is the space where I can love you, and you can love me. Crossing boundaries disrupts that."

Zeilah knows that the Lord loves her just as she is. She says, "He made me as I am. I feel that He is not going to take it away—that He looked at me and said, 'That's good. You're good.'" When she got married she decided that when she is attracted to someone, she will tell her husband, not harbor a secret attraction. "I'm a lesbian. I am going to be attracted to women, whether it's a physical or emotional attraction. I watch that I don't fantasize about someone; I'm conscious of it. I don't pretend to be anything other than what I am." Her acceptance of herself, combined with a focus on her desire to keep covenants and act in her marriage with integrity, enables her to live with self-honesty and self-acceptance.

Lydia observes that "living in full awareness of who you are is better than living in denial." Lydia is right. I worked in therapy to unpack the decades of shame and false narratives about myself, my relationship with God, and the best way to respond to my attraction to women (Pro Tip: forty years of denial ain't it). I have a list of reminders for "Inner Work" that I keep on my phone. As I read and reread these bullet points, I begin to replace my unhealthy narratives with an approach that invites acceptance, gentleness, and honesty.

My Inner Work

- Be with the feelings to learn from them
- Be able to be messy without judgment
- When feelings come up, try to understand them and sit with them
- Be observant, curious, and non-judgmental
- Keep intention to have God here
- Learn how to sit with feelings in the space between cravings and aversion

- Don't get lost in the craving or run away in aversion
- The more I hate—or fear—something, the more power I give it
- There can be things I like/enjoy; because of my values I feel it, but I don't get lost in it
- Be curious for the purpose of understanding, to act from a position of power

Every one of those points is a golden nugget for me. These phrases became the new narrator of my experience, replacing the "if they knew you, they wouldn't like you/God will never be pleased with you/you are bad" narrator who got booted to the curb.

When I left for New York City to help my daughter, Mark told me to "notice when I'm noticing." I wasn't noticing women at that point. But when I started to feel scared and alone and angry, I began to notice every woman who jogged past me on my evening walks. I noticed their beauty, their strong bodies, and suddenly I knew what "notice when you're noticing" meant—it prompted me to turn to my inner work and, first, stop judging myself. I knew what I was feeling, but why? I started to see patterns in times of stress and in times of loneliness. Because I was replacing self-judgment with curiosity, I could learn from a gentle inner environment, and the tsunami of shame receded without doing its usual damage. The less shame I felt, the less I hated myself, and the less I feared what these feelings meant for my eternal future. I was more aware of God's love and guidance. I became able to draw on my own power to respond rather than react, and space began to grow for understanding and honesty.

SELF-HONESTY IS THE FIRST BOUNDARY

Boundary work helps me to become a differentiated person, less vulnerable to merging with others. I recognize my protective feelings as a huge red flag that tells me to back off and let the other adult take care of herself. Most of the women I interviewed had clear limits they had learned to integrate into their relationships with other women, and their insight is deepening my own awareness of how to create healthy relationships with boundaries.

I also learned that wanting to have an exclusive friendship or feeling jealous were both red flags that I was merging with someone or feeling entitled to her. In contrast, wanting to include others in our circle of friendship, and recognizing that I am not jealous of my friend's other relationships, reassures me that my feelings for that friend are within my boundaries. Even if I feel intense love for that friend, I can relax into it because it doesn't have the signs of an unhealthy and undifferentiated relationship.

Other women have recognized the specific boundary needs that are important for them. Jane hugs with one arm but mostly doesn't hug. Touch is hard, but that may be from childhood sexual abuse—she has to remind herself there is safe and healthy touch. "Honesty with my spouse is the biggest thing. If I'm interacting with someone on a regular basis where I have feelings for her, I tell my husband, 'It's this person, this is what I do, this is what I feel. If I'm working with this person, this is how often we're around each other. She gets my heart beating. I'm not confessing, just sharing.'" If she doesn't talk about it to him, it gets messy in her head and warps the truth.

Early in their marriage, they went to her friend's missionary homecoming. As they got out of the car, Jane said, "I need to tell you something. I need your help; make sure I'm never alone with my friend. We had a bit of a relationship in college, and I'm still really attracted to her. I need your help. I don't want to hurt you." He responded, "I can understand, she's so pretty." That gracious, non-judgmental space from him made it possible for her to feel safe being completely honest with him.

Wendy distinguishes between what is sexually relevant to her and objectification. If she notices an attractive woman at the beach, she asks herself "Do you feel entitled to her?" If entitlement is not there, she's not objectifying, it's just sexually relevant to her. She can observe her awareness of a woman without judgment or getting pulled into it. Boundaries are what allow her to be confident in her relationships and know she is not disrupting or objectifying healthy friendships. Her boundary strategies include putting her phone on airplane mode at 11 pm so she doesn't have late-night text conversations. If she wants to keep something a secret, that's a red flag to her. Secrecy gives feelings more power. She is honest with her husband, and his past history suggests he will be gracious and generous.

McKell is honest with friends if it feels like they're starting to cross boundaries, being clear about what she wants. "This is what I need: we're texting too much, we're texting too late, we're being too flirty. I'm married, and I don't want anything to distract me."

Zeilah builds a group of healthy friends, realizing that because of the dynamics of her marriage and her husband's limited ability to connect emotionally, she has to go outside for emotional connection. She "happily and mindfully seeks out connection and joy" to fill her relationship needs without crossing boundaries that God has set through her covenants.

River is honest with herself and others, and she quotes a saying from the Navy Seals: "'You will not rise to the occasion, you will fall to the level of your training.' Just saying you have boundaries is not enough; you need to actively think about, plan, and figure out what to do in advance," she says. "That is your training. Plan and run scenarios in your head. Boundaries aren't static, they require constant work."

In my reading about boundaries, I came to understand that there should be some sort of consequence attached to a boundary violation: "If *that* happens, then *this* will follow." I always thought of the consequence as some sort of punishment, such as new restrictions for a period of time. In contrast, River sees boundary injuries as an opportunity for more learning. She attaches consequences to her boundaries, but they are not punishing. If she expresses affection in a way that crosses her boundaries, she might read a book on building healthy relationships, as she works to learn from her mistakes. She creates consequences that aren't negative but lead to more growth. "Boundary work enables me to have healthy, emotionally fulfilling relationships with other women while protecting my relationship with my husband. Honesty is the essential condition."

Cindy set her boundaries a long time ago: "I will never compromise someone's life. I will not cause someone else to falter."

One of my friends shared, "At one point I came close to crossing boundaries with my friend, so I went in and talked to my bishop about what was going on and what we were struggling with. That conversation was very empowering and really helped. When my friend and I were borderline inappropriate, we received a deep sense that God gave us each other as a gift. Talking to someone was the right thing to do." She learned in Twelve Step meetings that "you are only as sick as the secrets you keep." She was able to keep her best friend by protecting her boundaries.

A consistent theme with all of this boundary work is the need for absolute self-honesty about feelings, motives, and behavior. Boundaries can create safety, but what about the underlying pull toward women? If my attraction to women is not all bad, is it possible there is some good in it? Mark challenged me to find the gifts that are in these attractions. That was surprising, but intriguing. Wendy explains the need to be loving and affirming to ourselves: "This is the thing you need to say to yourself: It's okay that you love women. It's okay to love that about yourself."

RECOGNIZING THE GIFTS

In all my prayers over the years, I had never asked for my feelings for women to be removed. When a friend suggested that I could pray for that, it instantly felt wrong to me. There is more to my being gay than just a romantic desire to be with a woman. There is something fundamental to my soul, and even though the shame was toxic to me, the shame didn't come from God. Being sexual with another woman would break my covenants, and I don't want to do that. But I find there is some part of my love for women that is good; that feels so much a part of me that praying to have it removed it would diminish me. God is in this somewhere, and I have resolved to find the good that comes from my attraction to women.

Our dark side is our light side under stress. I had seen and feared the dark side, but what was the light side, the gifts from God that under the influence of the Spirit would transcend the natural and become sanctified to God's good will? I began to ask "What part of this helps me to become more like my Heavenly Parents? What interferes?"

I thought of my service to women—my compelling desire to support them and to encourage their growth. That had been expressed through formal service in Young Women and Relief Society but also through visiting teaching or mentoring or ministering in ways that were inspired by God. I love connecting with women through scripture study, and so I did that informally with friends and through teaching Sunday School, Relief Society, and the stake institute/adult religion class for young moms.

I was drawn to Twelve Step support groups, and I was eager to help the women in those groups find hope and healing through deepening their relationship with God. All of these relationships and ways of serving women are grounded in healthy same-sex emotional and spiritual intimacy that honors the covenants I made with God. These friendships are emotionally satisfying and allowed me to use my gift of deep feelings for women in ways that glorify God.

I also found a gift in the suffering that brought me to the Savior's feet. My struggles, my fears, my grief, my confusion, my anger, my sadness—all eventually brought me to the Savior seeking healing for my shattered heart. Talking to my family and others about my same-sex attraction required stripping away self-protection and every last vestige of pride. I approached in complete honesty and total surrender to kneel at the Savior's feet. I came to know God's love in a way that is worth all that I have sacrificed and suffered. I replaced false narratives about the nature of God with an awareness of His loving-kindness, patience, and mercy for me. I have learned I need never be alone in either my rebellion or my submission—He will stay by my side through it all. As I continue to feel strong attraction to women from time to time, I can turn to Him and tell Him exactly what I am experiencing, and He will listen with compassion.

That awareness and acceptance of God's love for me enables me to feel empathy and grace for others. As I became less harsh in my self-judgments, I looked at others with greater compassion. Sister Barbara B. Smith teaches, "In Spanish, the word *charity* means 'the love that never ceases to be.' In Micronesia, the word love translates into 'the power to change lives.' These tender nuances give us a better understanding of the pure love of Christ. As we serve with the single desire to nurture all life, we come to know what charity means."[2] My understanding of God's love expands, as does my ability to love.

My openness about my same-sex attraction doesn't just bless me; my friends and ward members are increasing in love and grace for me and other LGBTQ Saints. I believe the presence of LGBTQ members in our ward and branches is a blessing to all who are willing to open their hearts and minds to a deeper love for each of God's children.

I had dreaded the possibility of a mutual romantic attraction to a friend. When it happened, I found that God got there first and prepared a way for me to learn and heal. I began to build skills and trust for myself, to set healthy boundaries, to know myself better, to recognize and nurture the gifts that come with my orientation toward women, and to come one step closer to loving as God loves.

Notes for Chapter Ten

1 Dieter F. Uchtdorf, "Come and Belong," *Ensign*, May 2020.

2 Barbara B. Smith, "The Bond of Charity." *Ensign*, November 1980.

Chapter Eleven

WHAT IS THE DESIRE
OF MY HEART?

Mark invited me to develop a mantra to ground myself in my own identity. It is a key to differentiation, an antidote to merging with others. Merging (also called codependency and enmeshment) happens when our borders are too porous, and we merge with another person's emotions and need, because we are not secure in ourselves and our self-identity. My goal was to become highly differentiated, so I could sit with a person in high emotion and stay in a state of open-heartedness, not enmeshed but also not retreating. If I am connected to a higher sense of self, I see feelings, I sort them, but I am not sucked in by them.

When I start to feel my boundaries slip, or sense that I am over-identifying with someone else, I find I am taking on their thoughts and feelings, or trying to fix, rescue, or control them. My personal mantra pulls me back to my own side of the road. It didn't come easily. Mark suggested I write a statement consisting of two to five sentences that answer these questions:

- What is the ideal space I want to live out of?
- What do I want?

Out of these questions, I sought to craft a statement I could connect with multiple times a day to keep me grounded and prevent merging with others.

I worked for weeks to distill down the essential truths and desires of my life into a few sentences. Amidst so many conflicting choices, longings, aspirations, and roles, getting to the core of myself was a struggle. Looking back on my life and analyzing my choices was most helpful. This wasn't about who I wished I could be; my goal was to come to know and describe myself, not prescribe the *Ideal Meghan*. I wasn't searching for "shoulds." This was an exercise in coming to know myself as I am, the most true description of self.

I added some questions that helped me evaluate my past choices:

- What do I always come back to?
- What centers me?
- What is the consistent desire of my heart?

Looking back on my life, I could see that whenever I strayed from God and His covenants, I always came back, and I came back quickly. At one point in high school, I decided I didn't want to be lukewarm in my commitment to the Church. So I dropped it—completely, and for less than a week! I discovered that I couldn't stop praying and pretend He didn't exist. In deciding to get off the fence, I initially jumped to the wrong side, but it was a short stop. Like the earth circling the sun, I knew God was at my center, and His light and love were consistently the desire of my heart.

As I identified other constants in my thoughts, desires, and passions, I would bring draft versions to my meetings with Mark. He only made one suggestion—that I add something about my same-sex attraction. My first response was "That is not a significant part of my life!" Then I realized how much it had shaped me: my mental health; my internal narrative; my barriers to honesty with myself, God, and others; my faith in Christ; my complicated relationships with men and women and ambivalence in friendships. It seemed to touch so much—and I knew that though my relationship with SSA might change, I had never believed it would simply go away. It merited a mention too. I also wanted my mantra to reflect the theme of my daily work, the things I was drawn to spend time on, many of which focused on inviting others to Christ. I realized that my love and gratitude for Jesus Christ had become one of the organizing principles of my life.

After weeks of tweaking, I settled on six sentences. My relationship to women ended up claiming its appropriate amount of space:

- I am a disciple of Christ.
- I am faithful to my covenants.
- I love and cherish David and my family.
- I move through the world in a way that reflects humility and invites others to come unto Christ.
- I experience same-sex attraction, but it does not define me.
- My love for women manifests best in a commitment to help them gain a profound awareness of their own nobility and their potential to become like our Heavenly Mother.

Reading through my final version, it rang true. This was me! (Others might raise an eyebrow at "humility," but it is a desire of my heart, and I'm getting better at it.) This captured my essence, and as I repeated it throughout the day, I felt more and more grounded in who I was and what I wanted. It was also a valuable lens through which I could examine my relationship with my friend. If I became involved with her, what would be the end of the road? All I could see was destruction; I knew I would always return to God and my covenants, but in the meantime so many people I love would be hurt and relationships destroyed. The mantra was a valuable tool to take me out of imaginative, wishful thinking and ground me in the reality of who I was and what I really wanted.

Crafting this self-description required me to ask questions about the internal forces that shaped my life. I had wondered if staying in my marriage and in the Church meant I was suppressing my authentic self. Instead, I found those choices were manifestations of my authentic self. It described me in the same way a portrait captures both the image and soul of the subject.

BECOMING DEEPLY HONEST WITH OURSELVES

The development of a personal mantra is an exercise in self-honesty. It is also an exercise in honesty with God, requiring a willingness to become completely open. Our expectations may block that openness, especially if we anticipate condemnation or disappointment or disgust from Him. Letting go of those expectations allows us to become teachable and open to hearing His voice. Ultimately, finding an authentic self is based on not only our circumstances, gifts, and passions but also what we want to do with them—where we want them to take us—what we really want, not what we feel we *should* want.

Wally describes the importance of overcoming the expectation that she has to do everything perfectly so God will love her. She lived most of her life without self-respect or confidence in God's love for her, but as she began to heal and become more honest about her same-sex attraction with herself and others, her shame lost the hidden space it needs to thrive. Now she has the best relationships of her life with her husband, with Heavenly Father, and with herself.

Marisol describes how her bishop taught her to focus on her objectives, not her circumstances:

> I was trying to prepare my papers for going on a mission and working in a restaurant with a girl who was bisexual. We became really close. I liked being friends with this person but didn't know if there was more. I decided to talk to my bishop, and then I realized all the girls I had liked in the past. My bishop asked "Are you doing anything with this girl? No? Then it's not a problem. You can't get in a bubble and run away every time. This will happen more often. Stay there and have faith; if something happens, meet with me and we'll figure out what to do." I was really confused—why is he not telling me to leave? If my job is not a holy place, how do I stay here? [Sometime later] I had a dream where I heard a voice saying, "You need to stay and wait a little more." I came to realize a holy place can be my mind, my heart, and my intentions.

During the weeks that I crafted my personal mantra, I began to understand that I could look inward to find God and a holy place. Each of us has a God-given gift of agency and self-determination, and my discussions with other gay women show me that my expression of self is mine alone.

"When the Lord created us, He didn't do it with cookie cutters," River says. "He doesn't want us to cut off some part of ourselves so we can fit an image." Growth doesn't come through mindless adoption of someone else's framework. It comes through struggles, mistakes, learning, and sacred moments of recognition. It comes by learning through our own experiences. It comes through acting in the way that seems most congruent with our integrity and the desires of our hearts, looking inward for truth and upward for light rather than outward for advice and opinions.

COURAGE TO ACT

Growth also comes through being willing to take risks. What am I risking? I am surrendering the kind of relationship that feels most natural to me for nurturing relationships that are aligned with my values and goals. I am risking living in a duality of spaces that may blow up in my face. But this is my space—I feel the truth that I can be a gay woman married to a man I love and committed to covenants that put relationships I sometimes want outside of God's bounds. This space feels right and good to me, even if it's not always comfortable, and even though it looks different from others' paths.

Twelve Step principles come in, yet again, to support me each day:

- Let go and let God
- Keep it simple
- One day at a time
- Acceptance is the answer
- Progress, not perfection[1]

All of these are dependent on a partnership with God in which I am a full partner, an active partner, a partner with a voice and a choice and the right to learn from my experiences.

Mae told me she thinks that perhaps "this life is less about choosing the right and more about choosing. He cares more about us actively using our agency than always getting it right; what is important is choosing and acting. There is more learning that happens later." Mae points out the responsibility to be agents who act, and who act intentionally.

Elder David A. Bednar describes the importance of acting intentionally in our lives: "As you and I come to understand and employ the enabling power of the Atonement in our personal lives, we will pray and seek for strength to change our circumstances rather than praying for our circumstances to be changed. We will become agents who 'act' rather than objects that are 'acted upon.'"[2]

God wants us to take the risk to choose rather than recoil in paralysis from the risk of mistakes. Elder Lynn G. Robbins reinforces this when he says, "Repentance isn't the backup plan in the event we might fail. Repentance is His plan, knowing that we will. This is the gospel of repentance, and as President Russell M. Nelson has observed, it will be a 'lifetime curriculum.'"[3]

I've modified my mantra from time to time since its creation—not significant changes, just tweaks as I learn and grow. As I make choices, I get it wrong, back up, repent, and try again. In the process, I learn more about myself and about how God teaches me, and it enables me to be an agent who acts, learns from experience, discerns more clearly what she wants, and is better able to make future choices in alignment with those desires.

The COVID-19 pandemic and resulting changes in Church services gave me time to examine what elements of my Church experience bring me closer to God and what is an obstacle to a more intimate experience with Him. Taking the sacrament, attending the temple, singing hymns, and loving and serving others deepen my connection to Him.

I recognized, however, that overdependence on the structure and leaders of the Church had become a crutch for me. My fear of making a mistake resulted in looking to others to tell me the right answer. Rather than seeking to "Hear Him," I often simply sought my leaders' counsel and opinions. I was falling short in my personal responsibility and covenant of obedience to God, which required closer attention to His personalized tutoring. At the end of a BYU Devotional address, Elder Dallin H. Oaks stated, "As a General Authority, it is my responsibility to preach general principles. . . . I only teach the general rules. Whether an exception applies to you is your responsibility. You must work that out between you and the Lord."[4] I decided to be more engaged in seeking to hear God's direction in how to personally apply general guidelines laid down for a general audience.

FREEDOM TO SAY NO
EMPOWERS US TO SAY YES

This resolve was put to the test when I recently received a call to serve as Relief Society president in our young single adult branch. It came as a shock, and my impulse was to do as I had always done, as I had been instructed years before—to immediately accept. But instead I asked for time to pray and ask God about the call. I felt that there were a few things I should tidy up in my spiritual life. I did as I felt impressed to do, and after a few days I asked the Lord the same question I had been asking all week: "Do you really want *me* to do this?" I had started to open up to more people about my sexual orientation, and I thought of mothers in our stake whose daughters were attending our branch. What would they think about a gay Relief Society president? I was certainly in a transitional time for my faith, my attitude about myself, and the way I was going to be perceived by people around me. Maybe I wasn't the best choice?

I asked, one more time, "Do you really want *me* to serve as Relief Society president?" and I received an unexpected response: "What do you want?" First in surprise, then in self-reflection, I thought about what I did want. Eventually I answered, "I want to serve You and Your children and build the kingdom . . . may I serve as Relief Society president?" I felt both affirmation and acceptance.

I am struck by the fact that He really did give me the option to choose. The Lord didn't give me a choice between whether to accept His will or not—He asked for the desire of my heart. I recognized it, and then He allowed me to have it. I've heard we can't truly say "yes" until we can say "no." Over the past few months, I've come to a place with the Church where I could say "no" if I needed to without guilt, without fear of the Lord being angry at me. The acceptance was fully my choice (with His trust and invitation). The experience I had in this prayer/conversation with God was an affirmation of the power of recognizing my own heartfelt desire to serve God and saying a robust "Yes!"—not out of duty or obligation but as an exercise of my own agency and choice.

Recognizing we can choose what is best for us, rather than trying to figure out the single right answer on a multiple-choice quiz question, gives us breathing space to consider the outcomes we desire. I felt this from David when he told me he was *choosing* to trust me in our marriage. When he told me that, I didn't feel that I had to keep hustling for my worth and trustworthiness. I stopped worrying about earning his confidence, and it gave me space to relax and be free of the codependent need to influence his choices. His decision to trust me relieved me of the ruminating worry about what I merited, and I could attend to my own side of the street as I determined my own choices.

Moving through this process is both revealing and healing. Natasha found stability in the Church while she was making decisions soon after coming out. In time, she began to feel grief and anger because she felt she had no real choice. She stayed where she was out of fear, but eventually she realized she did have the ability and right to choose what she really wanted. With the freedom to leave, she found that she wanted to stay. She had a good relationship with her husband, and she was happy with her life. Having the freedom to exercise agency empowered her decisions to be her own and be satisfying to her.

Creating my mantra invited me to recognize what I really wanted as I worked to align my choices with the core desires of my heart. But that doesn't keep away the waves of attraction that sometimes seem to come out of nowhere. In those moments, I'm now more equipped to stay firmly grounded. A meditation teacher once recommended I ask myself, "Sweetheart, what is going on?" That kindness to self as I dig a little deeper keeps me in kind curiosity, not shame or self-condemnation. I now feel I am just as I ought to be, God loves me as I am, and I have more to learn, but I also know who I am and what I ultimately want.

It's not just healing that happens in relationships; it's also growth, empathy, and enlightenment. I found that as I became rigorously honest with myself and others, I began to see things as they really are, including myself.

Notes for Chapter Eleven

1 *Alcoholics Anonymous: The Big Book*, fourth edition (New York City, NY: Alcoholics Anonymous World Services, 2001).

2 David A. Bednar, "In the Strength of the Lord," BYU Speeches, October 23, 2001, speeches.byu.edu.

3 Lynn G. Robbins, "Until Seventy Times Seven," *Ensign*, April 2018.

4 Dallin H. Oaks, "The Dedication of a Lifetime." BYU Speeches, May 1, 2005, speeches.byu.edu.

Chapter Twelve

COMING TO KNOW GOD

My relationship with God started to change for the better during the time I was in Utah with my daughter, just after I talked to David for the first time about my attraction to women. I was in turmoil over covenants and grief and my future and my past. I felt so much anger, heartache, and fear. I directed all of it toward God. I wasn't reverent. I wasn't respectful. I was mad, and I swore at Him using words I'd never said in my life. I railed and raged and tantrum-ed like an ill-behaved toddler, and He responded as the most heavenly, patient parent. He didn't leave. The Spirit didn't flee, even when my language passed the bar for an R-rated movie. He stayed with me, He listened, and He *took it*.

I didn't deserve that grace. None of my good-girl, earn-His-approval behaviors were packed into the suitcase when I left my home in Michigan. I was nice to my daughter and her roommate, but once it was just God and me, it got ugly. And He still took it.

Now, I realize, why wouldn't He? Wasn't that the point of Gethsemane, to take it? To take it all, to let it weigh Him down so He could lift us up? I threw the worst I had at Him, and He didn't strike me down, upbraid me, or leave in a huff. He wrapped His arms around my shattered soul and wept with me. He didn't reject me for my sexuality or my contentious spirit or my foul language. He looked past all of it to the daughter who was in pain and needed comfort. I didn't deserve it, and that didn't matter. He gave it because of Who He is, not who I am.

The women I talk to are often in pain. During an anxiety attack, Marisol felt she was in hell. She received an impression from God "This is not hell, this is your Gethsemane, and Christ is next to you— He went to Gethsemane so He could be next to you." That is the nature of God.

LIVING WITH LOSS

It's easy to say "Just don't act on it" about feelings of same-sex attraction, but that dismisses the lifelong relinquishment of a longed-for relationship. Sometimes when I speak to a group, I will have a question something like this: "My daughter is in her forties and unmarried and a faithful member of the church. How is that any different than a LGBTQ member staying celibate for her life?" My friend Jenny answered this beautifully: "Your daughter can pray every day that she will meet someone and fall in love. A celibate gay member of the church prays every day that she won't."

God declares that "It is not good that the man should be alone (Gen 2:18), and psychology backs that up. Brené Brown says, "We are wired for connection. It's in our biology. . . . connection means thriving—emotionally, physically, spiritually, and intellectually."[1] Our Church teaches the primary importance of family, but choosing to surrender same-sex relationships can mean accepting a lifetime of solitude and loneliness, the equivalent of telling a straight person they can never, ever be partnered with someone of the opposite sex.

Elizabeth describes trying to "learn how to deal with grief and longing" for something she will never have. The experience of sorrow and loss is common among women who choose to stay in the Church—even if they are choosing what they want most, there is heartache for the kind of relationship they are sacrificing.

There is also grief over the complicated relationship between Church and sexual orientation/identity. In addition to pure doctrine, we may have been taught the opinions of men. Those can be harsh and may lead us to believe in an equally harsh God. Jessie describes thinking "if something is off, it must be me. But I'm coming to the realization that maybe everything that I was taught isn't absolute truth. Maybe I should rely on my faith and relationship with Heavenly Father more, which goes along with President Nelson's counsel to 'Hear Him.'[2] Having a firm foundation and a testimony means when things become rocky, I know where to turn for help; I fall on my knees and say, 'I don't know what to do with this.'"

GOD'S LOVING-KINDNESS

If we have been taught or imagined up for ourselves a God who is quick to anger, easy to displease, or impatient with our mortal struggles, then we are worshipping an idol in place of the living God. In Nehemiah we read of the God I discovered in my rebellious state:

> But they and our fathers dealt proudly, and hardened their necks, and hearkened not to thy commandments,
>
> And refused to obey, neither were mindful of thy wonders that thou didst among them; but hardened their necks and in their rebellion appointed a captain to return to bondage: but thou art a God ready to pardon, gracious and merciful, slow to anger, and of great kindness, and forsookest them not. (Nehemiah 9:16–17)

I wish I could start over and teach my children again. I taught out of fear—fear that if I didn't teach the consequences of sin, they would not choose to do good. I would do less warning today and more rejoicing. I would teach them of growth, repentance, joy, and the unfailing love of God. I would emphasize rules less and testify more of God's sweet grace.

God values our growth over fearful obedience. Adam and Eve transgressed and left the Garden, a place of safety, to venture into the telestial world where they could know "good and evil, and the joy of [their] redemption, and the eternal life which God giveth unto all the obedient" (Moses 5:11). The Fall blesses us as it brings about conditions that lead to joy. God's intent is to bring us into happiness, not to punish us for each misstep. If we treat every test as if it is the final exam, we won't make much progress, because learning generally comes through making mistakes and starting over.

The Lord often shows us the next turn without giving us the whole roadmap.

Wally doesn't know what the future is going to look like, but she is focused on doing the next right thing.

Jane describes how the Lord led her along by small steps to an unexpected event. She says it took about "four years before I felt something like [marriage to my male friend] would be possible. One time I had an impression as he was walking away: 'You will see those shoulders for the rest of your life.' Later I saw him at a friend's, as he came out of a darkened room, and heard, 'This is what he will look like when he comes out of the baby's room.' He was nothing like men who were sexually abusive to me growing up. I felt the Spirit telling me, 'Not every man wants to hurt you.'" Eventually her future husband asked her, "What are the chances of us getting married?" "Probably pretty good," she responded, though she was in love with her roommate. She was trying to have faith in things she couldn't deny and trust in the Lord's ability to prepare her for marriage to this specific man. She took each step as God led her to it, without demanding to see the whole plan at once.

At times we see the Lord reflected in the inspired actions of other people. I learned more about the nature of God from my husband, who gave me space to learn about myself and patiently waited for the outcome. David wanted me to choose him, but he didn't act out of constraint or control. He recognized I might not turn to him, and he still gave me space to come to my own decisions. I think it was a gift from God for him to have the wisdom and patience to do that, and I was able to see in flesh the godly attributes of patience and respect for agency. God also wants me to choose *Him*, but He will not coerce or force me. He offers me His love and trusts it will be sufficient to turn my heart to Him.

Stephen Cramer describes this love beautifully:

Christ has often demonstrated that His purpose is never to put us down or condemn us for our weaknesses or sins, but to save us from them, to strengthen and encourage us, to heal us of our infirmities and sorrows. . . . He has infinite tolerance, compassion, and mercy, infinite patience and forgiveness for every repentant person. There is never a trace of condemnation in His perfect and unwavering love. . . . God doesn't demand that we overcome every fault before He loves us, because He knows that if we need to change, discovering His love for us will lead us to change.[3]

Coming to know the true nature of God is essential to our salvation. In an earlier chapter I referenced *Lectures on Faith,* where Joseph Smith teaches that we need to have a *"correct* idea of his character, perfections, and attributes."[4] As I came to know God correctly, through both my peaceful and my tumultuous experiences with Him, my faith increased. The Savior asks, "For how knoweth a man the master whom he has not served, and who is a stranger unto him, and is far from the thoughts and intents of his heart?" (John 17:3).

TRUSTING IN GOD

Many of the women I interviewed described experiences that increased their trust in God and their understanding of His loving nature. Jen, a former drug addict, says "I see myself doing whatever God asks me to do. He rescued me from the depths of hell; I didn't deserve it, and there's nothing I won't do for Him. I see myself going forward in His hands."

Cindy is "continuing to pay attention to what God has in mind and stop assuming I have a clue what's in my future. I hope and want to pursue continued better thinking about what I can do for myself and continue to gain confidence."

Erin advises, "Don't quit praying. God is with you no matter what decisions you're making." That can contradict what we hear from family and Church members, but the lived experience of every woman I talked to confirms it. The Holy Spirit continues attempting to "entice" us even when we are at our most natural woman-ish, consistently inviting us to "become a saint through the atonement of Christ the Lord" (Mosiah 3:19).

God also promises that if we turn to Him and His love, He will sanctify our mortal experiences for our good: "And we know that all things work together for good to them that love God" (Romans 8:28). As we increase in wisdom through our experiences, God invites us to turn our hearts and lives to Him and allow Him to use "all things" for our good.

Jo describes how "experimenting upon the word" worked in her life. She was in same-sex relationships for much of her adult life. Periodically she would ask God in prayer and meditation, "Is this where I'm supposed to be?" Jo felt that God prompted her to stay in the relationship she was in at that time, and she felt that He would let her know when it was time for change. Many years later, when Jo began to feel that it was time for her to return to the gospel and the Church, she prayed to know if that was what He really wanted, and He confirmed it to her. "The Lord knows which of us will go on a circuitous path to discover the truthfulness of the gospel of Jesus Christ," she explains. "The Lord can work with our choices and will consecrate all of our experiences to our own good. Throughout our lives we will learn many things, and as we learn to align our will with God's, He will put our hard-won wisdom and skill to use in His kingdom. We will be able to serve others in ways we never dreamed."

Accompanying uncertainty is the truth that God knows what He's doing, and we can trust Him. Jessie says she lives by faith in God, because she realizes she can't predict her life moving forward. She explains,

> "I thought I could, but as I travel on this journey, I don't know. I trust that God knows where I'm going, and I will follow Him. President Nelson told us it would be impossible to survive in the last days without the constant guidance of the Holy Ghost in our lives. If we listen and follow Him, God will lead us where He wants us to go, and it's important not to judge others or the direction of their path. I have a strong visual of Christ walking on the water, Peter stepping from the boat to follow His invitation to 'Come,' and the other apostles shouting, 'Are you crazy?' Christ is out there and He's calling me on this specific journey; I just have to trust Him."

Because of the Atonement of Jesus Christ, there needn't be any failure—just learning. He loves me because I am His, not because I deserve it. What do any of us deserve, except death and hell? He wants to give us so much more than we deserve, including a rich mortal experience full of growth that helps us to know Him and become more like Him. He asks us to trust Him, ask Him, hear Him, and accept His love for us.

Notes for Chapter Twelve

1 Brené Brown, *I Thought It Was Just Me (But It Isn't): Women Reclaiming Power and Courage in a Culture of Shame* (New York, NY: Gotham, 2007), 122.

2 Russell M. Nelson, "Hear Him" *Ensign*, May 2020.

3 Steven. A. Cramer, *Draw Near Unto Me*, (American Fork, UT: Covenant Communications, 2001), 22.

4 Joseph Smith, *Lectures on Faith: Delivered during 1834 and 1835 to the School of Elders in Kirtland, Ohio* (American Fork, UT: Covenant Communications, 2000).

Chapter Thirteen

FINDING GRACE FOR FELLOW SAINTS AND LEADERS

I am sharing a story, sacred to our family, about a time when the priesthood and temple ordinances were not available to all worthy men and families. I am not relating this story as a precedent for change to Church's policy on same-sex marriage. What I do want to explore are the principles that have guided my relationship with God and His Church.

When the missionaries started to teach our family, I was the first to be baptized. My dad hesitated, even though he believed what we were hearing was truth. This was in 1972, and the church's policy at that time denied priesthood and temple access to members of the Church of African descent. My dad could not join what he saw as a racist church.

But he felt the Spirit when the missionaries taught us about the restored gospel of Jesus Christ, and so he took his struggle to the Lord. As he prayed about what to do, he heard the Lord tell him to be baptized and promised he would see the policy change in his lifetime. There was no explanation of why the policy existed, or how long he would have to wait. Just instruction and a promise.

Because of his willingness to act on the Lord's instruction, our family was able to be sealed in the temple. We embraced the gospel with all our hearts, and we grew, served, and matured in our understanding. Six years later, we heard the announcement of the revelation extending priesthood blessings to all worthy members, regardless of race. We were filled with joy for all God's children and with gratitude for the fulfillment of the promise made to my father.

Dad was serving as an ordinance worker in the Salt Lake Temple at that time, and he was teaching a class after work at a community college. One of his students was Joseph Freeman, who became the first man of African descent in the twentieth century to receive the Melchizedek Priesthood and be ordained an elder. When Joseph entered the temple, my dad didn't know he was coming but was serving at a place in the temple that enabled him to assist Joseph in entering the Celestial Room. The Lord blessed my dad abundantly for his willingness to accept confirmation without explanation.

I'm not sharing my dad's experience with waiting for priesthood and temple covenants to be extended to black members because I think it's a precedent for accepting same-sex marriage. We expected that the priesthood policy would change—the debate was about timing. Concerning LGBTQ individuals, mortal reasoning might lead me to decide there are only two possible resolutions: either we all become "fixed" in the eternities, or the doctrine will change to allow same-sex marriage in the temple. I think both of those "reasonable" solutions fall short of the perfect and compassionate plan God has for His children.

Instead, I believe that God's eventual explanation of the LGBTQ role in the Plan of Salvation is going to be creative, brilliant, unexpected, and entirely congruent with the nature of God, including His love, mercy, and justice. For now, I can rest in God's confirmation that He loves us exactly as we are; we have gifts and purpose in His kingdom; He has a plan for each of us to be happy; and greater light and knowledge will come in time. I trust in confirmation without explanation.

AN ONGOING RESTORATION

I learned three important lessons from my dad's experience that are relevant to my journey. First, the Restoration is ongoing. Two months after the announcement of the revelation in 1978, Elder Bruce R. McConkie gave powerful perspective at a BYU devotional:

There are statements in our literature by the early brethren which we have interpreted to mean that the Negroes would not receive the priesthood in mortality. I have said the same things, and people write me letters and say, "You said such and such, and how is it now that we do such and such?" And all I can say to that is that it is time disbelieving people repented and got in line and believed in a living, modern prophet. Forget everything that I have said, or what President Brigham Young or President George Q. Cannon or whomsoever has said in days past that is contrary to the present revelation. We spoke with a limited understanding and without the light and knowledge that now has come into the world. . . .

We get our truth and our light line upon line and precept upon precept. We have now had added a new flood of intelligence and light on this particular subject, and it erases all the darkness and all the views and all the thoughts of the past. They don't matter any more. . . . It doesn't make a particle of difference what anybody ever said about the Negro matter before the first day of June of this year.[1]

That perspective on the Restoration as continuing rather than complete is reinforced by President Russell M. Nelson, who states "We are witnesses to a process of restoration. If you think the Church has been fully restored, you are just seeing the beginning. There's much more to come."[2]

I expect more light and truth on the subject of LGBTQ children of God, and I believe it will come in an unexpected form that will make perfect sense when it is revealed. His ways and thoughts are beyond my ability to predict, though I know I can always trust in His good intent for me and His willingness to guide me on my unique journey through life.

SPECULATIVE EXPLANATIONS

My second lesson came as a result of watching church members attempt to explain the original policy on race and the priesthood. We do ongoing damage in those attempts. The policy ended in 1978, but efforts to justify or explain it by speculatively assigning motivation to God or leaders creates more pain even today. I continue to hear discredited explanations offered up as "reasons," when the reality is we don't know the mind and will of God or the full events surrounding the decision in the nineteenth century. Those explanations based on human logic and reason fall short and do unintended damage.

I feel the same when I hear people try to explain their views on the "causes" of same-sex attraction and gender dysphoria in a gospel context, to show where Church doctrine should change, or to speculate on the resolutions that will come about after this life. Mortal solutions are short-sighted when compared to God's compassionate, omniscient, and perfect plan, even though we have to wait for the veil to be lifted to reveal it.

Members may try to create clarity for themselves by explaining causes for same-sex attraction or gender dysphoria, proposing solutions to "fix" people now or in eternity, or predicting eternal outcomes. Without those comforting answers, we are left in a place of uncertainty and tension between what we know and what is unclear. That is where I live, and it's a great place to express faith. As Anne Lamott says, "the opposite of faith is not doubt, but certainty. Certainty is missing the point entirely. Faith includes noticing the mess, the emptiness and discomfort, and letting it be there until some light returns."[3]

CONFIRMATION WITHOUT EXPLANATION

The third lesson is the one I fall back on most: I can receive spiritual "confirmation without explanation." The personal revelation to my dad not only reassured him change was coming but it also let him know God is in charge and has a plan. It invited him to enter into a covenant relationship with God and trust Him in the things my dad didn't understand. I can look back and see the same evidence in my life. The Spirit gives me peace or instruction without a full understanding of how my experience fits into and advances God's plan for me. It is frustrating; I'm sure as a child I drove my mom crazy by asking "why" repeatedly. I want all the reasons. When the Lord doesn't give them, when He just says to me, "Peace, be still," I try to accept that He is at work, and I know I can trust Him.

I wrote earlier of the harsh criticism I heard in my youth about homosexuality that caused me to bury my sexual orientation because

I wanted to stay in the church. Many of you may know those quotes well. I heard them in real time, sometimes sitting in the Tabernacle. They were part of general conference, popular books, my seminary classes, Sunday School, and the culture of my young life. They caused great pain and trauma in too many of us.

But I also had one-on-one experiences with two of the leaders who were most vocal about homosexuality. My mom had worked for years at a local newspaper where one of the apostles was a senior editor before being called to full-time Church service. After I joined the church, we were visiting Utah, and my mom took me up to his office to meet him. They visited for some time about news-related topics, then I got to pose a question. I was a bit in awe, but I gathered up my courage, and asked what he thought about watching TV on Sunday (I was twelve, and that was top of mind for me). He kindly considered my question and thoughtfully answered that his family always enjoyed the Wonderful World of Disney together on Sunday evenings. I was satisfied with the answer, but I also came away with a feeling of being loved and seen.

Eight years later, David and I and my parents were waiting at the recommend desk in the tunnel leading from the Church Office Building parking lot to the Salt Lake Temple. It was our wedding day. As we stood there, the Prophet and President of the Church came up. He had just performed the marriage of one of his granddaughters. He took my hands and held them in both of his as he earnestly spoke to us about our future life together, and he then blessed us and our marriage. It was a beautiful, sacred moment. He is the same man whose book and talks are vilified by some for the way he spoke of LGBTQ people.

I share these stories because they give me important context. I felt nothing but love and goodwill from each of those men. They were not malicious. I can believe what they did or said was out of concern for the members of the Church and out of their limited understanding. Nephi teaches us that the Lord "speaketh unto men according to their language, unto their understanding" (2 Nephi 31:3). The Lord Himself says that He "giveth unto my servants in their weakness, after the manner of their language, that they might come to understanding" (D&C 1:24). I think "language" must include context, ethos, culture, even mistaken "facts" that are accepted as truth—for example, that being gay is a choice, an act of rebellion. If that "false fact" is a basic premise, then the reasoning to follow from that faulty premise will be invalid and untrue, even if the intent is good.

GRACE FOR IMPERFECTION

I have come to the point where I can give grace to well-intentioned leaders whose teachings were affected by the beliefs of their time. President Kimball, the prophet of my youth, asked God questions about race and the priesthood that challenged the status quo. Questions and increased understanding about same-sex attraction were coming later. The Lord invites us to hear the words of the prophet "in all patience and faith" (D&C 21:5), and Joseph Smith later wrote "I told them I was but a man, and they must not expect me to be perfect; if they expected perfection from me, I should expect it from them; but if they would bear with my infirmities and the infirmities of the brethren, I would likewise bear with their infirmities."[4] I speak differently today than I did forty years ago, or even ten years ago, and so do our leaders.

The church's distinction between same-sex attraction and same-sex behaviors and the recognition that same-sex attraction is not a choice didn't become clear until decades after my adolescence. Those changes came as we received more light and knowledge. Today the Church's position that "individuals do not choose to have such attractions"[5] gives more space for my attraction to women. When we change our perspective from "it's a choice" to "it's not a choice," it results in a paradigm shift that invites empathy and understanding rather than judgment, internally as well as from the Church.

Unfortunately, not every leader and teacher in our wards and branches is up to date on current Church teaching about same-sex attraction, and so the old teachings persist and continue to do much damage.[6] The Church is currently providing many resources that will help us to deepen our understanding, but busy and overburdened leaders may not have found them. One example is the Counseling Resources page for leaders on the Church website. Valuable insights there include

- "Feeling same-sex attraction or choosing to use a sexual identity label (such as gay, lesbian, or bisexual) is not a sin and does not violate Church policy."
- "The most important thing you can do after an individual discloses feelings of same-sex attraction is to listen and help them feel welcome."
- "Reassure them of God's love. Admit you may not fully understand what they are going through. Let them know you love them and want to understand."[7]

Efforts to explain spiritual causes or speculation about the next life are useless and often harmful. Telling LGBTQ people that they will be "cured" in the next life is doctrinally unfounded and can be an unwitting invitation to them to end their mortal existence prematurely. Repeating discredited theories about what causes same-sex attraction or gender dysphoria is at best a misguided attempt to help and at worst a cruel display of ignorance.

I don't have answers for all my questions. But I know where to turn for insight: to One who does have all answers, and He listens to me. He gives me what I need in the moment I need it. That may be just the reassurance that I am where I should be and to keep moving forward. He doesn't show me the whole roadmap and the reason for the route I'm on. But He tells me that He loves me, that I am just as I should be, and that all will be made clear in time.

Francine Bennion's talk, "A Latter-day Saint Theology of Suffering" is worth reading in its entirety, but here is one section I return to consistently; it helps me to feel forgiveness for the words and people who have and do hurt me, and it invites grace for myself as I am learning and doing better:

> Because of our ignorance and inexperience, we are hampered by things we don't understand and also by things we assume we do understand. What other persons have taught us, whatever their intentions, may hamper as much as help us. One of my prayers to my Father is that my children will be healed of my ignorance and will not bear forever the difficulties caused by things I have mistakenly done or not done as a parent. As I think of the atonement of Christ, it seems to me that if our sins are to be forgiven, the results

of them must be erased. If my mistakes are to be forgiven, other persons must be healed from any effects of them. In the same way, if other persons are to be released by the atonement, then we must be healed from their mistakes. . . .

. . . Of the very few things I truly know, the most certain, drawn from the most vivid and inexpressible experience of my life, is this: God is love, and our becoming so is what matters.[8]

I have hurt others and been hurt through good intentions. As I continue to heal through the love of Jesus Christ, I am better able to let go of anger, pain, and bitterness.

HEALING OLD WOUNDS AND SEEKING MORE LIGHT

The women I talked to have all struggled with reconciling their faith and their sexuality or gender identity. Elizabeth relates that her sexual orientation "has been a very big spiritual challenge for me. I've always been very faithful and trusting and feel like I've been obedient. But I feel conflict with sexuality and spirituality—what will I do? What will I choose? [I've read how some of] God's prophets have talked about this. . . . How could prophets write that? My relationship with Christ has grown through [asking these questions]."

Lydia believes "there can be great power in compassionately acknowledging the probability of closeted LGBTQ+ members among us, within our wards, family, and friend groups. . . . I was touched when a sister teaching the lesson specifically gave gender dysphoria and transsexuality as an experience that those around us might be having and as an added instance when we should all be truly welcoming of everybody and demonstrating pure love as our Savior does."

We can do better in reaching for that ideal. "I can't say that I've ever felt included based on my sexuality," Michele observes. "Maybe occasionally I've felt loved despite it by very close friends, but I've always been seen as damaged, broken or even sinful (not because I had sinned, just for preferring women) by the Church and members in general, including any bishops I've tried to talk to about it. On the other hand I have never read or heard any prophet or apostle say anything on this topic that has made me feel anything less than a cherished daughter of God. It seems to me that the message isn't getting through to the members."

More light comes as we are prepared, both individually and as a people. When I was younger, there were elements of the temple endowment that were confusing and painful to me. As I continued to attend the temple, taking my questions and hurt to the Lord, He taught me about myself. I asked if I, as a woman, was a second-class member of the Church. Was my contribution less necessary and important than a man's? Do I play an active or passive role? How does He feel about me? Heavenly Father gave me added nuance and perspective that prevented me from misinterpreting my temple experience until the ceremony shifted to align more completely with what He revealed to me about my place in His kingdom.

I also gained valuable insight from my experience with the missionaries when I was investigating the Church. I grew up as a Catholic, and I was taught that everyone has to be baptized to be able to go to heaven. But in some cases, babies died before they could be baptized, and so they would spend eternity in limbo (my apologies for simplifying a complex doctrine; this was my understanding from second-grade catechism). I was so bothered by those tragic babies; it was not their fault there was not a priest nearby, and it seemed arbitrary and cruel to punish them forever. It didn't fit with my personal experience of God, even at eight years old. But there was no solution—baptism is essential to return to heaven, they didn't get it, and it was all a terrible, faith-challenging tragedy.

A few years later when I learned about baptism for the dead during the missionary discussions, everything clicked into place. God's love became compatible with His justice, and I was amazed at this creative and unexpected solution! I've felt that amazement over and over in my life as He steps in with a brilliant and unanticipated resolution to an impossible puzzle. I expect the same as we increase in understanding about the Lord's resolution in the Plan of Salvation for His LGBTQ children.

I have worked on the pain and shame in my life that was the result of limited understanding and, at times, a lack of compassion. I can give grace to others as they learn (and help them out if they are ill-informed). While I will probably carry some emotional scars for the rest of my life, I am able to let go of active anger and bitterness most of the time (occasionally it flares up unexpectedly in a Church class when I hear those obsolete teachings repeated). I trust in the Atonement of Jesus Christ to heal me, give me peace, and correct all the wrongs of this life. And I watch and wait, knowing that the Lord has much more to reveal.

Notes for Chapter Thirteen

1   Bruce R. McConkie, "All Are Alike Unto God," BYU Speeches, August 18, 1978, speeches.byu.edu.

2   Russell M. Nelson, in "Interview with President Nelson and Elder Stevenson in Chile," Church Newsroom, YouTube video, 30 October 2018, 5:09–6:28, https://www.youtube.com/watch?v=hOc2R2IpK7w.

3   Anne Lamott, *Plan B: Further Thoughts on Faith*, (New York, NY: Riverhead Books, 2006).

4   "Joseph Smith's Feelings About his Prophetic Mission," *Teachings of Presidents of the Church: Joseph Smith* (2007), available at churchofjesuschrist.org.

5   "Same-Sex Attraction," from bishopric counseling resources manual; available at https://www.churchofjesuschrist.org/study/manual/counseling-resources/same-sex-attraction?lang=eng. Retrieved April 28, 2021.

6   See appendix for a summary of obsolete teachings vs. current teachings.

7   "Same-Sex Attraction," from bishopric counseling resources manual available at https://www.churchofjesuschrist.org/study/manual/counseling-resources/same-sex-attraction?lang=eng. Retrieved April 28, 2021.

8   Francine R. Bennion, "A Latter-day Saint Theology of Suffering" from BYU Women's Conference March 28,1986, available at https://www.churchhistorianspress.org/at-the-pulpit/part-4/chapter-43?lang=eng and in the Gospel Library App under Restoration and Church History > Women's History > At the Pulpit > 43. A Latter-day Theology of Suffering: Francine R. Bennion. Retrieved April 28, 2021.

Chapter Fourteen

TO BE SEEN AND HEARD

"Why do you have to talk about this?" Spoken or not, this question is a common reaction when a person opens up about their sexual orientation or identity. People may find the topic distasteful and uncomfortable, so they want to avoid it. They might wonder why it's necessary to share such a private matter: advancing an agenda for doctrinal and legal challenges? Trying to be trendy? Bringing private sexual desires and/or encounters into public view? It's damaging when others assume negative intent or reduce the meaning of what we are sharing to a simplistic cry for attention. Generally, "coming out" is more about healing and trust than advocacy.

If you are one of the blessed few who is trusted enough to receive this gift of vulnerability from someone, know that it is probably not the opening salvo in an organized attack on religious/cultural values nor a desire to latch onto the topic of the day. There may instead be years and years of struggle leading up to the moment of feeling safe enough to invite others into a sacred confidence.

Recently I began to feel a more insistent invitation from God to be open about my orientation, to write about it, and to talk about it. This was obviously a challenge for my family to accept—it felt risky and like it would take us further into the unknown. One of the ways in which I responded to this invitation from God, with the whole-hearted support of my husband David, was through recording an episode of Ben Schilaty's and Charlie Bird's podcast *Questions from the Closet*[1].

When I received a text from Ben letting me know my episode would drop in a few days, I went into a panic. I had been so nervous when I recorded the podcast that I couldn't remember anything I said, so I didn't know what was coming, and I was scared of the effect on my relationship with my children. I sent out a "help" message to my friends, telling them what was happening and asking them to pray for my kids. I didn't want to do more damage to our relationships than I already had, and this was a podcast that some of my children's friends would hear. It exposed our family in ways I knew would be painful to them. I also knew I had responded to a prompting from God to do the interview, and I pled with Him that my obedience to His command would not work to the permanent injury of my family.

My friends responded with prayers and reassurance, and when I listened to the podcast, I sounded more coherent than I remember feeling. I listened with raw nerves for anything that might hurt, offend, or anger my children, and I felt relieved that nothing jumped out at me. I honestly didn't know if any of them would listen to it, but at least they wouldn't have friends calling them and saying, "Is this your mom? Did you hear what she said?" I made an effort from the time they were teenagers not to embarrass my kids, and having their mom talk publicly about her sexual orientation blew that rule to pieces.

I was surprised and touched when first one daughter, then another, listened to the podcast. They were gracious in their responses, and it's probably the most concentrated gospel teaching they've heard from me since I was their seminary teacher! It actually started to open doors of understanding that had been stuck for a while. One of my girls told me she decided to listen as far as she could, and she ended up hearing the whole thing. There were parts of my story she hadn't known, and those pieces helped her to have a more complete and empathetic understanding. Something eased in our relationship.

This experience is evidence to me that God's ways are higher than my ways, and His thoughts higher than my thoughts. Mortal reason and fear told me that I would make things worse for my children by talking publicly about my sexual orientation. My limited faith had me praying that it just wouldn't cause irreparable harm. But God created a healing experience out of it. I was praying for damage control, and the Lord gave us grace.

In general, responding to the Lord's invitation to "open my mouth" and share with others, whether individually or more broadly, has been a healing experience for me. The suffering I've experienced as a result of the incongruence between my orientation and what I was taught at Church have had a profound impact on my life. Opening up to those around me takes down barriers and increases trust and unity. I'm not flaunting sexual desires; this is not all about sex. It is fundamental to the way I relate to women and men on an emotional, intellectual, and spiritual level.

Jo says she spent a lot of time "trying to tease apart the spiritual and temporal parts of being a gay woman because being a gay woman is more than just the physical or sexual attraction to other women. I can still consider myself a gay woman and keep my temple covenants and the law of chastity."

My attraction to women doesn't feel like a mortal affliction. Could this be a core part of who I am, both a gift and a challenge but not something "inflicted" upon me? That makes sense to my head and my heart. I am grateful for the way the gifts of same-sex attraction bless my life and help me to serve God and His children.

I have heard Church members express their belief in the healing power of the Atonement of Jesus Christ for all afflictions and their subsequent confusion over the lack of "healing" for members who experience same-sex attraction. They are mistaken about what needs to be healed. I experience the healing power of the Savior as He takes away my shame, my fear, and my sorrow over my orientation. But as I stop viewing my orientation as an affliction, He is able to open my eyes to see the power and blessing and gift of it.

I know many people who are LGBTQ and devoted members of the Church. If faithfulness was a condition for becoming straight, they would qualify. I don't think God is intending to change my orientation. Instead, He is changing my understanding of who I am and the glorious future He has for me as a gay Latter-day Saint.

COMING OUT OF HIDING

When I come out from hiding and shame, I open a window into a sacred part of my soul, and I ask to be seen in ways that matter deeply to me. It is love and acceptance that are needed, not suspicion or judgment about motives, or misguided promises of change for the faithful. I don't need to be fixed or rescued—I have a Savior for that. I just need you to listen and see me and sit with me.

Of course, families want to fix what they fear. They want their loved ones to have a future that reflects all the wonderful blessings of life and discipleship. They want missions, marriages in the temple, grandchildren, and trials overcome through faith. They may need to privately grieve the loss of their dreams, even as they are reassuring their child, spouse, or parent of their love and support.

My children's stories are theirs to tell, not mine. But I will say that I have learned a lot from the mistakes I made when I first talked to them about my orientation. David and I should have talked to them together; his presence would have reassured them that we really are united moving forward. I did start by telling them that I was not leaving our family or the Church. My intention was to stay in both, and they needed to hear that because they had not seen or known any Latter-day Saint women who came out as gay and stayed. I said the words, but my body language communicated fear and shame, and it spoke so loudly it drowned out the feeble words tumbling out of my mouth. It was a traumatic evening for all of us, and healing from that has come slowly and sometimes in unexpected, podcast-driven ways.

A few years ago, I told my children I wanted to be more open about my sexual orientation. It was hard for them to understand, but my daughter who had recently finished active treatment for breast cancer said that when she meets new friends, she realizes that if they are going to be close, she needs to tell them about her cancer experience. "If you don't know this about me," she said, "you don't really know me." I'm not implying that having cancer is like being gay— rather, the key point is that when I am willing to invite others into a vulnerable, tender, and formative part of my life, I am inviting friendship on a deeper, more trusting level.

As I began to open up to my friends about my experience with same-sex attraction, I came out of hiding and allowed myself to be seen. "If you don't know this about me, you don't really know me, because it impacts me in so many ways." My willingness to open up and invite others into the sacred spaces of my heart required courage and trust and felt like a massive risk, even with my closest friends.

The time came when I realized that if I wanted people to hear my story from me, rather than another source, I needed to speak out. I was writing about my experience, and I was going to be presenting at the North Star Conference and sharing my story on the podcast *Questions from the Closet*. I knew it was time to be more open with my friends and family.

I reached out to a wise friend, Travis Steward. Travis is about my age and served as a bishop, in stake presidencies, and as a mission president before he began his own journey to acknowledge his same-sex attraction, open up to his wife and others, and begin to reconcile this hidden part of himself with his life and faith. When I heard him and his wife interviewed on Richard Ostler's *Listen, Learn, and Love* podcast, his life resonated with my own.[2]

I eventually became friends with Travis and his wife Margaret, who is a brilliant woman of great faith. I reached out to them when I felt it was time for me to invite others to see this part of me, and I asked them for advice. One of the things Travis suggested was to identify my pain points and put my initial efforts there. I knew immediately what he meant. My biggest fears were telling my mother, my brother, and my mother-in-law. When I open up to friends, even though they are important to me, if they reject me, I will recover. But these key relationships in my family carried a much higher risk. I knew if I told them, I could tell anyone.

Shortly after talking with Travis, I wrote a letter to my mother and brother. I felt a letter would give them time to process and talk to me when they were ready. I also joined David on a video call with his mom. My mother said that when she prayed about my situation, she received the answer "Just love her." I felt love and acceptance from my family, and that made it possible for me to open up to many more people.

The following week I sent this message to friends and others I had worked with or taught over the years:

> I joined the church when I was eleven, and my commitment to being a disciple of Christ has shaped my life ever since. It is still the most important aspect of who I am, and my relationship with God is the one I most treasure—just ahead of David and my family. I am grateful for their love and support of me.
>
> I have likely shared my testimony of Jesus Christ and His gospel with you. I may have shared some of the struggles of my life, but I have not opened up to you about my feelings of same-sex attraction. It has been a constant throughout my life, though for decades I buried it under a mountain of denial, shame, fear, and depression. About seven years ago I admitted it to myself, and then to David. The years since have been filled with pain, joy, and personal growth for both of us. David and I have become much closer since I have been able to be honest and let down walls of shame and self-protection.
>
> As I have gradually opened up to a few people, I have been able to come out of hiding and begin to breathe. To be seen and still feel loved and valued is one of the greatest blessings of my life. Being open about the reality of my orientation is not self-indulgent or attention-seeking; it is my willingness to invite others onto sacred ground. I know I have no control over how you respond to this email and to me, but I invite you to choose a desire to understand, rather than condemnation or rejection.
>
> I love the gospel, and I am committed to building the kingdom. As an expression of that, I have been able to help other LGBTQ members feel their worth and believe in God's love for them. That message is one I feel called to share more broadly, and over the next few months I will be writing and speaking in public ways. Because of that, I wanted to share this message with you, today, and I want you to feel free to talk to me, ask questions, and let me be a resource for you to gain more understanding for LGBTQ Latter-day Saints. If you want someone to talk to about your loved one's experience with same-sex attraction, or your own, I am a safe person.
>
> Thank you for your friendship. I hope my honesty and openness strengthen rather than diminish it.

The outpouring of love and support I received was overwhelming. Some friends responded with vulnerable stories of their own. I felt a deeper bond to people I had known and worked with for years. David Augsburger explains that "Being heard is so close to being loved that for the average person, they are almost indistinguishable."[3] When people are willing to hear and see me, I can feel their love for me.

There were also a number of people who didn't respond. Maybe they needed some time to process or maybe they felt I should have kept this to myself. It doesn't matter. I didn't do it for them. When I sent the letter, I tried to let go of the outcome. I felt I could take deep, unguarded breaths for the first time in memory. Perhaps my inviting others in was beneficial to them—I hope so—but it was an act of healing for me.

INVITING OTHERS TO SEE US AND HEAR OUR STORY

Telling others and being seen is such an important and healing step for LGBTQ members of the church. Elizabeth says she would like to be open and honest because "people in church don't have much empathy for us, but they'll never develop it if they don't know about us." Many of the discussions at church or among friends may refer to "them" without realizing that group includes "us," perhaps even a dear friend sitting in the room who has never felt safe enough to share her experience with anyone.

Women who are bisexual may be more likely to have their experiences dismissed and their motivations for coming out questioned. Lydia is a bisexual woman who says that because she is married to a man, the other side of her sexuality gets lost in the mix. Her family members are most likely to overlook or set aside her sexuality, saying, "We don't see you that way. Are you sure you need that label?" She feels seen in part but not in whole. "It's been a fundamental part of my life experience, it's a piece of how I relate to other women and to men," she explains.

Phoebe had similar conversations with family members and friends at Church who ask, "If you are also attracted to men, why do you even need to talk about this?" She can be happy and satisfied in her marriage, she says, but it won't make attractions go away. It's part of her, and she wants to stop feeling shame and depression because she can't be open and express what she's experiencing to someone.

After Elizabeth came out to her family and friends, a family member pulled her aside and told her that everyone believed she would leave her husband. She was asked to prove that would not happen. The uninformed assumptions of family members were painful and resulted in unrealistic demands. Elizabeth loves both the Church and her husband, but how can she provide sufficient proof to warrant her family member's approval? She and her husband need the love and support of their family rather than their skepticism.

Marisol observes that "when people make an effort to understand me, it makes a huge difference. They think they need to give people answers, but they just need to understand." This is reinforced by the instruction on the Church website to leaders, family members, and friends. Leaders are advised, "The most important thing you can do after an individual discloses feelings of same-sex attraction is to listen and help them feel welcome." After reassuring them of God's love for them, these possible questions are suggested:

- Will you please tell me more about your experience?
- How have these feelings affected your life?
- How have they affected the lives of your friends and family?
- How can I help you?[4]

Those questions create safety for more discussion. People don't have to be instructed on Church standards, policy, or doctrine for same-sex attraction. They can probably recite it. What they don't know is if you can still love them, and they need your reassurance at that moment and in the future.

Whenever I opened up to a friend, I would experience a huge vulnerability hangover afterwards. I would often second-guess my decision. I needed to hear from them the next day, just to know we were still friends. It also gave them a chance to regroup, if they had been surprised (or shocked), and engage in the conversation again with a clearer head. I always appreciate someone coming back to the topic. It feels really odd if we talk about it once and then never refer to it again. That reinforces shame.

Among the women I interviewed in mixed-orientation marriages, several had told their husbands about their attraction to women before getting married. There seems to be a connection between the way their future husbands responded to their disclosure and satisfaction in their marriage relationship. Some men were dismissive of the women's same-sex attraction, feeling that it wouldn't be an issue once they were married, that it would go away once they were in a sexual relationship together, or simply that it was easiest to pretend it wasn't there. These men tended not to ask any follow-up questions or show much empathy. This disinterest about something so central to their wives' inner lives damaged the relationship.

Zeilah's future husband told her "I'd be a fool to let that stop me," but he didn't ask any questions and didn't want to discuss it. He didn't really understand the implications, she says, and it has been a huge problem in their marriage.

A few husbands, whose wives told them years into their marriage, felt threatened and insecure. They were suspicious and checked up on their wives regularly, imposing boundaries that restricted the women's ability to feel trusted or free to exercise their own agency. Instead of protecting the marriage, that response undermines the mutual respect for agency that is essential to a successful relationship.

Another group of men responded with empathy and curiosity, choosing to act in a way that reflected trust and support as their wives navigated their experience. On their fifth date, Lydia's future husband asked her about past boyfriends, and she told him that for years she was attracted to her best friend who was straight, so she hadn't dated many guys. He gave her a hug and said, "Thank you for telling me; what has that been like for you?" Later he said, "I have so many questions, I hope you don't mind." Lydia says he understands her life experiences, when it's been hard for her, and how much the LGBTQ community means to her.

Elizabeth had been married several years when she decided to unpack her attraction for women and "figure it out." She had feelings for a friend and thought, "It's not fair to him—if I felt that way toward a man, I would tell him." Her husband is her best friend, and she tells him everything. So she told him she had feelings for a friend and wanted him to know. She said she thought she might be bisexual.

"Don't worry, I have this under control, it's fine," she told him. "I still want to hang out with my friend; do you care if we still walk?" He replied, "I trust you, it's fine." When it was no longer a secret, the feelings for her friend lost their power. "Now he knows every part of me, and he still loves me. His reaction," she explains, is a "huge and beautiful example of unconditional love: here is something that is painful for you to hear, but you still show love."

Natasha had a similar experience when she shared with her husband. Talking about it and being open helped her become a happier person. She says, "I am right in my skin. I make sense." All of her relationships are better because she's happier, she says; she was not herself before, trying to be someone else.

Feeling "right in my skin" is a great description of the feelings of honesty and authenticity that come from opening up to people who are close. That is one purpose of "coming out." I am a committed Latter-day Saint in a mixed-orientation marriage, so most acquaintances assume I'm straight. Unless it's relevant to the conversation or relationship, I don't need to correct them. But there is another good reason for being more vocal.

DIVINE INSPIRATION TO OPEN OUR MOUTHS

I've been surprised at the number of women who say they are feeling a strong prompting from the Spirit to come out of hiding. Mariah and her husband separately experienced that impression the same day, and when they talked about their experience in tears that evening, they both felt fear about what it would mean for them and what possible consequences might follow. They have been married for years, their children are grown, and Mariah could continue to pass as straight with friends and family. But the call to share their experience was too compelling. Theirs is one of many stories with the same pattern of feeling prompted to talk about their same-sex attraction, acting on that invitation in spite of the fear and uncertainty that accompanies it, and finding peace in, as Mariah says, "following what God prompts you to do, even if it's uncomfortable." She hopes for greater self-acceptance and to offer help to women who are still hidden.

I would probably be happy just telling close friends that I'm gay and leaving it at that—but how many women out there are alone with this, thinking they are the only faithful member of the Church who is attracted to other women? How many friends and family members lack insight into the lives of their LGBTQ loved ones? Could my existence and my voice challenge Latter-day Saints' misinformation about gay members of the church? I recently saw a comment on a Church Facebook post saying, "There is no such thing as an LDS/LGBT." While the comments section of Facebook may not be a measure of common attitudes in the Church, it does reflect a great deal of confusion about how and where gay members fit in. Where there is misinformation or a lack of information, negativity rushes in to fill the gaps. Could my story help to change the perspective of people who are misinformed?

Ironically, I've heard LGBTQ allies make a similar claim that there is no place in the Church for LGBTQ members or that it is impossible to stay active in the Church. This not only warps the attitude of members toward someone who may come out as gay in their congregation, it also creates fear in the women who are active members of the Church and privately aware of their attraction to women. When they look around and can't find anyone like them, they have no idea of their path forward. What does that mean for them? Do they really have to leave the Church? Do they really belong? Our visible presence at Church helps create an awareness that it can be a welcoming place where LGBTQ members can feel we belong. As we work together to create a safe and welcoming space, perhaps fewer members will feel they have to leave.

For years, I didn't know anyone who was gay in my Relief Society or in my stake. My family members were distressed to learn about my feelings for women because the only women they know who came out as gay also left the church and their family. It is comforting for me to see someone like me at church, to be able to share common experiences and insights. The more we create safe space for others to begin to be open about their lives, the more we can understand the varied experiences of all God's children.

If a friend trusts you enough to share their orientation or identity with you, you can create a safe space for them by recognizing the faith that has been placed in you—tread lightly and with love in the sacred spaces of their heart. Recognize that talking to you is an important part of their healing and self-acceptance. Ask "What has this been like for you?" and listen without trying to teach or advise. Follow up the next day to reassure them of your love and respect. They need to be seen, heard, and feel your ongoing acceptance and love.

Notes for Chapter Fourteen

1   Meghan Decker, "Is It Ever Too Late to Come Out?" *Questions from the Closet*, 2021; available at https://podcasts.apple.com/na/podcast/is-it-ever-too-late-to-come-out/id1504990147?i=1000532257879.

2   Richard Ostler, *Listen, Learn, and Love*, podcast; available at https://www.listen-notes.com/podcasts/listen-learn-love-hosted-by-richard-ostler-KJGsTky7cE1/.

3   David W. Augsburger, *Caring Enough to Hear and Be Heard* (Ventura, CA: Regal Books, 1983).

4   "Same-Sex Attraction," from bishopric counseling resources manual; available at https://www.churchofjesuschrist.org/study/manual/counseling-resources/same-sex-attraction?lang=eng. Retrieved April 28, 2021.

Chapter Fifteen

ALTERNATE ROADS

Several months ago I started interviewing the women whose stories I've been quoting. I capture each of these women in a freeze-frame, at one moment in time, and there is still a lot of life ahead of them. Since then, some of them have made major life decisions that have altered their intentions or relationships. Some are choosing to stay in the Church, some are in a same-sex relationship, and a subset of them wants both. These are stories of holding conflicting desires in tension. But the Spirit is present in the lives of all these women, and they all feel Heavenly Father's love and awareness.

Isaiah teaches us about the nature of "our God, [who] will abundantly pardon:"

> For my thoughts are not your thoughts, neither are your ways my ways, saith the Lord.
>
> For as the heavens are higher than the earth, so are my ways higher than your ways, and my thoughts than your thoughts. . . .
>
> So shall my word be that goeth forth out of my mouth; it shall not return unto me void, but it shall accomplish that which I please, and it shall prosper in the thing whereunto I sent it. (Isaiah 55: 7-9, 11)

Each of these women's lives look different, but they share one thing in common: they are reaching out to Heaven, asking for direction.

Some of them are not on paths that align with the standards of the Church. As I struggle to understand why others are led to such different paths than I am, I think of my mom, who resigned her membership in the Church when I was in my early twenties. She had remained a Latter-day Saint from her childhood through the first twenty years of marriage, even though my dad, brother, and I were all Catholic. Then she felt God call her back to the religion of her youth when I was ten. Eventually our entire family became Latter-day Saints, and we were sealed in the temple. Later in life she felt that God was prompting her to begin the long process of conversion to Catholicism.

At that time I was completely dismissive of her personal revelation. "God doesn't lead people out of covenants," I said to myself. "I don't know who she's listening to, but it's not God." Now I realize I put a box around God, constructed of my expectations and limited vision. I really don't know what He did or didn't say to her. I do know she was earnestly trying to hear and follow Him. She had important and faith-affirming experiences on that path, which don't make sense to me but which are real (she received a testimony of Joseph Smith as she was serving retired nuns in a convent). Today, rather than dismissing the experience that led her away from the Church and our family's covenants for a time, I finally acknowledge I don't understand all things. His ways are higher than mine, and His thoughts higher than my thoughts.

When one of my daughters left the Church, I received two messages from God. The first came in answer to my pleading prayers when He told me to be at ease and trust her to Him. The second came from a Relief Society teacher who described her fears for her son, then shared the instruction she received in answer to her prayers: "You love him, and I'll teach him." When I heard that, the Spirit carried its truth and peace into my soul.

Those messages worked together to bring peace to my broken heart and calm to my frantic mind. I didn't need to figure out how to rescue or fix or control my loved one. I could be at ease and trust God to work for good in her life, while I put all my effort into simply loving her as she is and trusting her to navigate her own life in the way that makes sense to her. That peace and calm allows me to get out of God's way, let go of my own agenda, and love with pure intent. She is now married, and she and her wife are happy. My husband and I are also happy, and though we are each on different paths of happiness, we can respect choice, love one another, and listen with empathy and compassion.

Joy is a lifelong member of the Church, returned missionary, and mother of many and is in a same-sex relationship. She has been dating her girlfriend for almost a year and they are each other's first same-sex relationship. Joy always planned on having a typical Mormon family, but after much pondering and prayer decided to date her friend, and she was just as surprised as anyone else when she took that step. She has already seen benefits, she says, such as feeling closer to God's love than she's felt in years, her children having another wonderful adult to give them time and attention, and a general sense of peace and wellbeing. She looks forward to seeing more benefits as time goes on. This has been a "healing season," and she senses Heavenly Father's love daily. She considers herself a friend to the church and plans to "stay in as far as they will let me." Her deepest desire is to worship Christ and treat others as Christ would.

Mae attends remote Church, watches general conference, and is also dating a woman she loves. Her hope is to be as active as possible, as much as the Church will allow. She loves the Church and loves the community. When I first talked to her, she was anticipating going to in-person church for the first time after COVID restrictions lifted; her girlfriend would be in town, and they planned to go to Church with her kids and see how they were received.

After she met her girlfriend, she prayed about what to do, and felt the direction to just love. She feels like Eve in the Garden, faced with two conflicting choices. When I checked in with Mae four months after our initial conversation, she talked of the pain and turmoil she feels in Church. Because she has been asked to refrain from making any comments in second hour, she feels isolated from the other sisters and like she doesn't belong anymore. She knew dating a woman meant she was forfeiting her temple privileges and the opportunity to serve in a calling or take the sacrament. But she didn't expect to be completely muted, especially since she would never speak against the Church's policies and doctrines in Relief Society or Sunday School. She explains, "I want to share my experiences with the Spirit, with

Christ, and I can't." The painful realization that her testimony of the Savior has been silenced makes Church attendance almost impossible for her.

As I listened to Mae, I could feel her sincere and good heart. While she and I have made different choices, hers was one of the interviews where I had the strongest sense of God's love for the person in front of me.

Joy has similar feelings about losing her voice in Church. She relates an experience in Relief Society: "When the teacher instructed each sister to go around the room and share one quick thing—[my partner and I] had to decline. When there were sign-ups to minister to other sisters—we had to decline again. When the sisters were scrambling to remember a quote—I had to stay silent even though I had it memorized, and it is hung on my office wall. We have been asked not to speak. A story from my mission popped in my head that I know the women would have loved—yet I must stay silent . . . from the beginning to the end of Church it is crystal clear we don't belong." While Joy knew she would not be able to give a talk or a lesson, her leader's decision to suppress her voice in classes was a blow that made it hard to believe there was any place her in Church.

Blake's biggest challenge has been to reconcile what she believes doctrinally with her orientation. When she came out in 2014, her resolve was "I'm in the Church. I've done it for thirty-six years. I'm staying in Church, and I'll be single the rest of my life." Her reconciliation process over the first few years was tough. There was a tremendous strain on her mental health. She felt suicidal, and though she knew wanting to be gone was not something she would act on, she still wanted to be gone so badly. She bookended her days with tears.

After a couple of years, she saw herself on the way out of the church, thinking "Maybe this isn't for me." She sat with that for two more years, going to church the whole time. She felt it was important to make the decision about staying or leaving the church while she was actively attending church. Then she had an experience that prompted her to sit down and think about her life as a whole. She pondered the scripture "Men are that they might have joy" (2 Nephi 2:25) and asked God, "Do I get joy, or is this only for straight people? Who is allowed to have joy?" She felt that God told her to live her life and find what brings her joy. She sensed that she could choose to be single, marry a man, or find a woman. She felt that God was giving her the option to follow the path that makes most sense for her.

When she started dating her girlfriend, she says "It brought me more happiness than ever before, and I went with it." She would like to have both parts of her life coexist, so she talked to her bishop about her presence in church. She did not ask for a temple recommend, a calling, or to take the sacrament; she just requested one square foot of cloth on Sunday where she can sit and worship. Her bishop responded with warmth and kindness, telling her he would not hold a membership council unless she wants one as a means to an end of restoring fellowship or temple worthiness. "Come, worship," he said, "you're not harming anyone by being here."

CONFLICTING DESIRES

The next three women are confused about their path forward. They are caught in the crossfire between conflicting hopes: the desire to be with a woman and the desire to be faithful to their covenants. As with the stories above, these are snapshots of a singular moment in time in unique lives.

After Eliza accepted her attraction to women, she decided she would stay single and in the church, and be good at it. She would "rock that aunt-life and be a good person." But when she eventually prayed and asked God about dating, she was shocked when she felt the encouragement to have the experience of dating women. All the women she has dated are active Latter-day Saints, and it's messy. She is distressed about the possible consequences of dating and partnering with a woman. Eliza wants to be as involved with the church as leaders will allow her to be, and she doesn't feel that her dating a girl is impeding her relationship with God. But if her ordinances were revoked, that would create a distance from Him. She feels comfort and anchoring in the knowledge that "He is aware and He knows how to solve this. He has a solution that works, He has power to create it." She has faith in God's love for her, and she knows He doesn't have mixed intentions for her.

Rebecca explained to her bishop that it's not just sexual connection that characterizes her attraction to women; it's emotional, spiritual, and multi-dimensional. The sexual attraction is magnified because of other attractions. "It's so immensely distressing that it's something I will never have," she says. As a young teenager, "I felt a spark when women touched me, so I stayed away from feminine touch. I have suppressed and been ashamed of this part of myself for so long. My sexual orientation feels integral to me, and I know now that I am beautiful because of it. I feel God telling me, 'It is beautiful, you don't need to be ashamed.'"

Disclosing her same-sex attraction was a hard blow to her husband. She told him her feelings were stronger for women than for men. He became anxious and clingy, so they started working with therapists individually and together, sorting through their feelings. They separated, and he went back to porn and emotional absence, while self-medicating with excessive tech use and distancing from their family. Life is difficult right now, and she is trying to decide what she wants. Grappling with wanting to pursue relationships with women and the likely consequences of that at church has led to suicidal ideation.

She talked with her bishop but left his office in intense turmoil. Her personal revelation and personal experience are in conflict with church policies. She says, "God wants me to love this aspect of myself, and shame makes that hard. My fear of rejection is poignant, the fear of how my church community will respond to me." Being gay is who she is, but the church teaches not to have a same-sex relationship, and she doesn't know how to make sense of the opposing forces. She says, "I can't understand why my fake, painful heterosexual marriage of fifteen years would qualify me for exaltation when a genuine, loving homosexual marriage would bar me from the kingdom of God."

A CIRCUITOUS ROUTE

Some of the women I talked to had been in relationships with other women and then returned to the church. Their stories don't represent the future path for all LGBTQ members who are in same-sex relationships. The women I spoke of earlier are not predestined to leave their girlfriends and wives and return to church. Each one of us has an individual, custom journey, and many women spend their lives in fulfilling same-sex relationships.

But these women who return to our wards deserve our attention, support, and profound respect. They are choosing a hard path, and our friendship will make it less lonely. Many of them feel they never left Jesus Christ or His gospel, but their church engagement was not aligned with their deep faith, and they have each felt called to return to the Church. These are often stories of supreme sacrifice, and more than once I found myself thinking of Abraham on the mountain with his only child, prepared to surrender whatever the Lord asked of him.

Between the time she was eighteen and twenty-four, River lost track of how many female romantic partners she had. She didn't like the monster it fed in her, and when she was about twenty-four she fell head over heels in love with a girl and got engaged. River says "To wake up in someone's arms and hear her thanking Heavenly Father that I am in her life—that is the ultimate relationship goal. Then Heavenly Father made it very clear that I needed to leave." Meeting her girlfriend had helped with her healing from childhood sexual trauma. When God told her to leave, she was also told she was past that point of healing and ready to change. She did as God asked and broke up with her fiancée.

Zeilah and Beth both had similar experiences of being called out of relationships with women. Zeilah was on her mission when she became attracted to a companion. After her mission, she moved in with her best friend. They were in love with each other but wanted to stay faithful to their covenants, so they kept dating guys. She talked to many bishops and characterized herself not as gay, but "just loved her." Her question to herself became "Will I leave the Church and be gay or stay in the church?" It was not a struggle between mind and heart, she says, but between heart and heart. She loved the Lord and her friend, and she didn't want to take her friend from the Lord or keep her from heaven. She eventually told the Lord, "If You require me to give her up, I'll do it."

Zeilah moved far away to try to separate. After three months of depression, praying and fasting to detach from the relationship, she felt the Lord communicate to her "I can see you're willing to give her up. I don't require that of you. You can have her in your life if you keep the relationship within the bounds I've set." She saw that the Lord would help her be who she is and also have Him in her life. She didn't have to choose between them. The Lord blessed her in unexpected ways to be able to change her relationship with her friend. He taught her, "You can be you, just as I made you. You don't need to give Me up to be you, just live in my boundaries." She says, "The Lord heals hearts, and He healed mine—He helped me love in the right way."

Beth's journey took her out of membership in the church and into a long-term relationship with her partner. As she began to come back to church, God sent her "hands that were easy to grasp." She understands how God feels about us because of the relationship she had with her stake president—there was so much love there. She had felt shame all her life, but the shame mostly left. She recognizes that she needs to put her faith in Jesus Christ. Shame is not the burden God wants her to carry.

She was rebaptized in 2018. It was a rough decision, because she knew she was going to be alone the rest of her life. Making the decision to come back to the gospel path has brought her the most peace of anything she has done. Walking away had brought her the most pain.

She wishes she had known the amount of peace she would feel when she came back. She experiences loneliness, but that emptiness is filled by Heavenly Father to a degree, and she can open up to the Savior. She knows she is right with Heavenly Father, even though it is hard.

Beth learned that Heavenly Father wanted her to use her agency and understand what it's like to make decisions that weren't influenced by other people. She fought before this life for agency. "I had to have the experience to know what the relationship was like," she explains. "Through exercising my agency, I could make the fully-informed decision to come back and know what I was surrendering." It is a source of strength to her now, as she feels a lot of loneliness. She doesn't think she could stay without equal knowledge of both paths.

Daniela says, when she's able to feel Heavenly Father's love, it decreases the feeling of fear and shame. "It's okay to not know all the answers," she says. "All I can control is the here and now. I don't have to solve eternity today. We work from here to eternity, not from eternity to here. A big mistake I made was I thought I knew how people would react. I took away their choice by not talking to them. I needed to let them come to terms with their fears and mourn the loss of their plans and expectations for me."

When she met her future husband, she really liked him and wanted to know right away how he would react to her orientation. She told him she had dated women, and she was involved in the LGBTQ community, then asked what he thought. He responded, "I don't care who you're attracted to, I care about who you decide to love. Let's make a deal that we'll be friends first, then see what comes." She says, "He gives me space to be myself. I tell him everything, but he gives me space to process things."

Cindy felt that she was where she belonged for the first time in her life when she started to engage with the gay community. She went through multiple relationships and grew into monogamous relationships, spending fifteen years outside the church. She didn't agree with a lot of the philosophies in the gay community, and she felt God was missing from her life. She began to reconnect with God, and that eventually led her back to the Church for the last twenty years. She is committed to living a celibate life; her goal is to stay close to God by studying and searching. She has just moved into a new area and would like to find a group of single people for friendships. It's hard to be single and not able to relate to people at church, she says. Having a "church friend" to sit with makes a little difference.

Many women are making choices to bring themselves into a covenant relationship with God and fellowship with the church, and yet they often feel alone in their efforts. At times they feel intense loss and loneliness. They are sacrificing every single day, and we can support them by inviting them to sit with us at church, go out for ice cream, or let us learn about their lives and offer real friendship.

None of these stories is complete. Beth observed that she feels comfort knowing she can change her mind at any point, and Heavenly Father will support her agency. When she was away from the church, she never left God. Beth says "If I were to leave again, I would find a way to experience God that would be equally beneficial and lead me to the same end. Choosing the path I have because of the sacrifice it requires causes me to feel His love for me and his gratitude for my willingness to choose this hard path."

When I initially interviewed her, Sky described her unbearable heartache when she dwells on the fact that she's going to be alone forever. Her story continues to unfold. Recently I talked to her, and she said, "When I look around and see how many people have stepped up and made themselves my family, I'm happier than I've ever been in my life."

We are eternal beings. Our stories and our growth extend both through and far beyond this mortal existence. Without knowing how everyone's story will play out, we can give grace to one another while we continue to grow, learn, seek happiness, and progress on our individual paths.

The prayer of Thomas Merton reminds me that the desire to please God is more important than living a flawless life:

> My Lord God, I have no idea where I am going. I do not see the road ahead of me. I cannot know for certain where it will end. Nor do I really know myself, and the fact that I think I am following your will does not mean that I am actually doing so. But I believe that the desire to please you does in fact please you. And I hope I have that desire in all that I am doing. I hope that I will never do anything apart from that desire. And I know that if I do this you will lead me by the right road though I may know nothing about it. Therefore I will trust you always though I may seem to be lost and in the shadow of death. I will not fear, for you are ever with me, and you will never leave me to face my perils alone.[1]

I see that desire to please God and find the right road in the lives of many of the women who share their stories. As we listen to one another, our hearts expand. Elder M. Russell Ballard issued this invitation:

> I want anyone who is a member of the Church who is gay or lesbian to know I believe you have a place in the kingdom and recognize that sometimes it may be difficult for you to see where you fit in the Lord's Church, but you do.
>
> We need to listen to and understand what our LGBT brothers and sisters are feeling and experiencing. Certainly, we must do

better than we have done in the past so that all members feel they have a spiritual home where their brothers and sisters love them and where they have a place to worship and serve the Lord.[2]

From the women I interviewed, I consistently sensed a desire to know and do God's will, to Hear Him, and to let Him lead through difficult and thorny paths. There is much here I don't understand, but one piece I am certain about—as I listened to these women, a window opened from heaven, and I received a glimpse of God's love for them. Every interview was a sacred experience, as they invited me into their lives, and I realized that God is working in each of their lives for good. I know with absolute conviction that He knows them and loves them.

As you've read about these varied experiences, you may wonder how to respond to gay members of your family and ward. What is the line between loving and condoning? It's helpful to examine the word "condone." It comes from the Latin *condonare*.[3] Depending on the context, *condonare* can mean "to refrain from punishing" or "to give a gift." That offers me clarity: If I am concerned about whether I am condoning wrong by welcoming a gay couple to sit in the seat next to me and join us for dinner, attending a friend's same-sex wedding, or using the preferred pronouns for a transgender ward member, I can ask myself "Do I have any responsibility to punish this person?" The answer is always "No," and I can instead offer the gift of my friendship.

When we talk to LGBTQ friends and family and hear their stories, we can determine best how to reach out to them. If they are lonely, we can open up our hearts and homes, and we can make a welcoming space on our pew. They may be afraid of losing our friendship to disapproval and judgment, but we can leave judgment to God and be a friend at all times and places. Mostly, we can listen with love.

Does it promote evil to listen and try to understand another person's life experience? I think we all agree on the answer: a resounding NO! Our covenants bind us to each other, to mourning and comforting and listening. At the very least, we can recognize the heavy burdens that our spiritual siblings may be carrying and be moved with compassion for them. Their stories will change our hearts and help us to understand how our Heavenly Parents will use us to bless the lives of these children They love so deeply.

Notes for Chapter Fifteen

1   Thomas. Merton, "The Merton Prayer," *Reflections*, January 1, 1970; available at https://reflections.yale.edu/article/seize-day-vocation-calling-work/merton-prayer.

2   M. Russell Ballard,. "Elder Ballard Tackles Tough Topics and Gives Timely Advice to Young Adults," BYU Devotional, Provo, UT, 14 November 2017.

3   From Latin *condonare*; see https://www.thefreedictionary.com/condone.

Chapter Sixteen

CREATING SAFE PLACES AT HOME AND AT CHURCH

One of the things I learned from my interviews with Latter-day Saint LGBTQ women is that lots of people are doing things right—families, ward members, and leaders. There are heart-warming stories of love and support that show us what best practices we can adopt in our own sphere of influence. Creating safe spaces is critical to the emotional and spiritual health of our loved ones and ward families. It is also instrumental in our own growth toward loving as God loves.

President Russell M. Nelson has emphasized the importance of gathering. The next step is belonging. Elder M. Russell Ballard explains,

> The Savior's invitation to come unto Him is an invitation to all not only to come unto Him but also to belong to His Church.
>
> The Mayo Clinic recently noted: "Having a sense of belonging is so important. . . . Nearly every aspect of our lives is organized around belonging to something." This report adds, "We cannot separate the importance of a sense of belonging from our physical and mental health"—and, I would add, our spiritual health.[1]

CREATING SAFE HOMES

The risk to mental health and suicidal ideation came up over and over again in my interviews. I belong to a local support group for Latter-day

Saint parents of LGBTQ children. One of the first resources we discussed was the Family Acceptance Project (FAP), an initiative that works to prevent physical and mental health risks for LGBTQ youth in "the context of their families, cultures, and faith communities." Members of the church helped to create this resource for Latter-day Saint families.[2] If a child is part of a family that is highly-rejecting of LGBTQ people, including a child in their own family, that child is

- *Eight* times more likely to attempt suicide
- Nearly *six* times more likely to report high levels of depression
- *Three* times more likely to use illegal drugs, and
- *Three* times more likely to be at high risk for HIV and sexually transmitted diseases.

Some of the highly-rejecting behaviors described by the FAP include verbal harassment because of a child's LGBTQ identity; excluding LGBTQ youth from family and family activities; blocking access to LGBTQ friends, events, and resources; and preventing the child from talking about their LGBTQ identity. There is a more comprehensive list in the pamphlet, and if you have an LGBTQ child, this is an invaluable resource.

Church leaders should encourage families to accept and love their LGBTQ children. President Dallin H. Oaks said, "[W]hat is changing—and what needs to change—is to help church members respond sensitively and thoughtfully when they encounter same-sex attraction in their own families, among other church members or elsewhere."[3] Elder Quentin L. Cook explains what that looks like:

> "As a church nobody should be more loving and compassionate. No family who has anybody who has same-gender [attraction] should exclude them from the family circle. They need to be part of the family circle. . . . [L]et us be at the forefront in terms of expressing love, compassion, and outreach to those and let's not have families exclude or be disrespectful of those who choose a different lifestyle as a result of their feelings about their own gender. . . . I feel very strongly about this. . . . [I]t's a very important principle."[4]

All of the women I interviewed are adults, but some still experience rejecting behaviors from their families. Tori says that after she came out and was divorced, her relationship with her mom changed dramatically. They used to talk daily, but now it's just occasionally. She wishes there had been a safe space for her growing up to "feel what I feel and have those feelings validated and heard. There is power in being heard. If I had felt safe enough to be heard, my outcome would have been different. I would have asked the questions I needed to ask rather than hiding."

Lolly says that had she been younger when she came out, "I would have been much healthier, and I might have handled depression differently." Jessie has a similar perspective; she recently lost a lot of weight and says, "When people ask how I did it, I want to say I was shedding shame. If only they could see what is happening internally—a miraculous transformation through self-love and acceptance because now I *know* God loves me, exactly as I am. He loves me because He created me."

Self-love and acceptance can be experienced at home if children are in a positive environment. The FAP describes accepting behaviors that we can adopt, including listening respectfully; expressing affection when your child tells you or when you learn that your child is gay or transgender; supporting your child even when you may feel uncomfortable; requiring that other family members respect your LGBTQ child; and welcoming your child's LGBTQ friends into your home. These types of behaviors create a space where a child may experience love and acceptance, so they can begin to feel that acceptance for themselves. It also builds faith that God loves them.

A few of the women I talked to describe a resilience developed in their homes. Jo grew up in a Latter-day Saint home. Her mother comes from a family legacy of generations of strong, educated women who championed other women. Jo listened to her mother's stories of the women she came from, and when Jo realized she was gay as a young teenager, she saw that one of the spiritual gifts that came with her sexual orientation was a strong desire to love, understand, and further the women around her. She wanted to see them succeed and be strong. Jo could see how she was a lot like the women she descended from and her sexual orientation didn't change that and, in fact, helped her deepen her love and understanding of women.

While Vanessa's home was not explicitly gay-friendly, her family's experience living in different countries abroad developed an appreciation for diversity. They were willing to learn new languages and appreciate new cultures, and that influenced Vanessa's being "comfortable with the fact that sometimes I'm attracted to men, and sometimes to women."

In our homes, our wards, and our neighborhoods, we can model our behavior on this guidance from Elder Marvin J. Ashton:

> Charity is accepting someone's differences, weaknesses, and short-comings; having patience with someone who has let us down; or resisting the impulse to become offended when someone doesn't handle something the way we might have hoped. . . . The best and most clear indicator that we are progressing spiritually and coming unto Christ is the way we treat other people.[5]

A SAFE SPACE AT CHURCH

Robin has only had positive experiences with anyone she's come out to at church. When she has talked about being gay, ward members have come up and thanked her for sharing her story and her faith. Her biggest challenge is knowing that staying in the church means she's going to be alone. She explains "I live in this irony all the time where the most important thing is family and eternal marriage. I want that more than anything, and it's the only thing God has told me I can't have—not in the way I would need it." She loves the temple, and her relationship with God through the temple has brought her the most peace in her life, but the sacrifice this requires is something she feels every single day.

We can recognize and respond with compassion to the pain of those around us. When I asked Sarah about her experience at Church, she said, "The Church causes me pain. I'm in a different category of human, and if other people knew about me, they might consider me perverse, unnatural, or just say 'How sad, what a trial.' For queer people outside the Church, it's not a big deal, just an interesting factoid about you. But at Church there is something wrong or pitiable about me. Outside of the Church people don't look at me like I have a terminal illness."

Jace, a transgender man, describes Church as being the place where he felt the most anguish, not the place where he felt the most love. He looked to Church members "for help, but received only judgment." Sarah and Jace are not focusing on their struggles with doctrine (though that does cause pain, too). They are talking about everyday interactions with other members.

Our commitments, especially at baptism, put us into covenantal relationships with one another. Alma said we promise to "mourn with those that mourn, and comfort those who stand in need of comfort." John the Baptist gave answers to his newly-baptized followers based on their specific circumstances:

And the people asked him, saying, What shall we do then?

He answereth and saith unto them, He that hath two coats, let him impart to him that hath none; and he that hath meat, let him do likewise.

Then came also publicans to be baptized, and said unto him, Master, what shall we do?

And he said unto them, Exact no more than that which is appointed you.

And the soldiers likewise demanded of him, saying, And what shall we do? And he said unto them, Do violence to no man, neither accuse any falsely; and be content with your wages. (Luke 3:10-13)

Is it a stretch to imagine that if we came to him saying, "We have gay members at Church, what shall we do?" he might answer, "Make room for them on your pew. Reach out to them in love. Invite them to dinner. Be their friend"?

President Dallin H. Oaks described our pioneer legacy as "a legacy of inclusion. We live in a time when inclusion is needed . . . as a church and as a culture, we need to lead out in demonstrating inclusion."[6] How can we be more inclusive of our LGBTQ brothers and sisters?

I heard these words repeated over and over: "I am lonely," "I've felt different and isolated from others since I was a child," "I don't belong here," "It's hard to feel that I fit in at Church, that there is a place for me." We need to create that place. Lolly said "People say [my presence is] too uncomfortable for members. Isn't 'uncomfortable' how people grow? I believe God created LBGT people in Church to teach other people how to love. As hard as it is for straight people to love me, it's hard for me to love some straight people because of how they respond to me."

The injury we cause may be unintentional or thoughtless. Vanessa describes sitting in Sunday School, hearing a negative comment about gay people, and thinking, "That's going to hurt someone."

Marisol shares similar thoughts: "Every time I heard someone talk about being gay in Church, it sounded like they lost their exaltation. We need to be more careful when we talk about things we don't have experience with—we don't know if something we say will be painful and hurt someone."

Leila Jane is afraid of not being able to serve in the Church or of being excluded from serving in Young Women or Primary. She has most recently been a member of her ward's Relief Society presidency, but now that she's out publicly, the fear is there. "How will the church limit my potential?" she wonders.

We can do better than dismissing or treating with contempt another member's reality. Jessie feels pain when members say, "It's okay to feel it, as long as you don't act on it." Not only does that lightly pass over the incredible grief and loss of "what feels like the most natural loving relationships, it implies that the feelings are wrong too, otherwise acting on them wouldn't be so bad."

"Everything will be better in the next life" is not a hopeful or full answer, Lydia observes. She would like to see changes in understanding and acknowledging how hard our teachings are for LGBTQ people because simply teaching the doctrine of marriage doesn't compassionately recognize what it means for them.

Some have heard family members or friends say that after intense prayer and seeking to know God's will for them, they have received direction to start dating and pursue a same-sex relationship. We may find ourselves wondering, "Would God ever give direction that contradicts Church doctrine?" Perhaps it's helpful to consider that, unless we are called as a Judge in Israel, we don't have to pass judgment on that answer to prayer. Jo states "So what if they said they received that personal revelation that seems wrong to us? For all we know, they did! It's called 'personal revelation' for a reason. To help make sense of this kind of situation, what we can do is focus on Christ's expectations of us and how He taught us to treat others. When someone is praying to know the way forward, and they feel as though they've received an answer from heaven, let's celebrate that! We all learn to hear the Spirit and the Lord's direction in different ways and at different speeds. So, as fellow Latter-day Saints, we can do more to support those who are making that effort and let the Lord (or their bishops) counsel them if they haven't gotten it quite right yet. When we show love and understanding, we invite the Spirit to be with us." The Spirit has access to us and can work through us to lift others when we are filled with compassion and empathy.

Elder John K. Carmack explains: "Because God and Jesus Christ alone can judge fully what is in people's hearts, they alone can wisely and perfectly temper justice with mercy. . . . It is for this reason we are admonished not to judge others."[7]

Elder Dieter F. Uchtdorf tells us we "simply have to stop judging others and replace judgmental thoughts and feelings with a heart full of love for God and His children."[8]

What does that look like? Sky was in a Sunday meeting when the stake Relief Society president commented that she had found North Star, and it was a great help to her in her relationship with her gay son. This leader accomplished so much with that one comment. She normalized talking about gay family members, and it carried additional weight because of her Church calling. She shared a resource with people who might be afraid to ask but could go home and privately look it up. And she helped Sky feel that there was someone who would accept her. After the meeting, Sky privately reached out to thank her and tell her about herself. That brief comment created a safe space for a lonely member to open up and be seen and lovingly accepted.

Lydia has seen families become estranged by the intolerance of some parents toward their LGBTQ children, and it breaks her heart. "I cannot imagine a response further from the limitless love and empathy of our Savior and Heavenly Parents," she said. "I think it is important to remember in our ward families as well, because we understand that we are all part of the same eternal family with our

Heavenly Parents and our Savior. Let us love each other as we want to be loved."

Fanny says, "Being married is such a critical part of exaltation, but being single doesn't necessitate repentance, so we can't fix it. So much of social connections are based on kids and husbands. Without that we don't have anything to talk about." She really appreciated being asked to teach Gospel Doctrine because it meant she was seen as a whole person. If she dated and found a permanent relationship with a woman, it would impact her membership, but nothing had led her to believe her ward would not find a way to make her feel welcome and find creative ways to involve her. "I feel seen in this ward," she says, "I am like everyone else. They are not evaluating me on my orientation or marital status."

Elizabeth shares a story of a Relief Society lesson that changed her feelings about belonging at church:

> I have been struggling lately with what I perceive as lack of empathy in the church toward LGBTQ people. Today we discussed President Nelson's talk about how the Lord can move mountains in our lives. We all wrote down the mountains that have been in our lives this past year. I wrote as my mountain "Reconciling my sexuality and my spirituality. Coping with the pain of sacrifice." All the papers were collected (this was anonymous) and read by the speaker. When she got to my card, tears welled up in her eyes as she read what I wrote. After she read it she said, "Wow, this sister has a lot of faith."
>
> I could FEEL that she felt a small portion of my struggles and even though she didn't know it was me, I felt SO MUCH love from her in that moment. That made a huge difference to me. . . . Even though I'm gay, I will still be loved by my sisters (or at least one) at Church. That felt really good.

Zeilah notes that her stake has luncheons for older sisters and provides Sign Language classes for people to support deaf members and help them feel welcome. She asks "Could we have an LGBTQ group? Could we be together and belong and have support? Officially seen and noticed by the Church? It's so lonely not being known or seen or supported through this incredible challenge [of being an active LGBTQ Latter-day Saint]."

Beth describes the power of hearing her local leaders acknowledge there are LGBTQ members in our stakes by speaking of them in inclusive ways in talks and lessons. She is grateful when "leaders speak up and correct when unkind things are said in reference to LGBTQ members. Having leaders do this is very important. I do this on a regular basis in my ward, and it gets exhausting by myself."

I had an experience at Church where dread turned to gratitude. I was in Utah to visit my daughter in June 2015, on the Sunday when a First Presidency letter was to be read to adults regarding the Supreme Court decision legalizing same-sex marriage.[9] When I realized I was going to be in Utah County for the reading of the letter, I admit that my biased thinking told me there would be a painful discussion to follow. I assumed there would be a lot of comments about the damage to our country and families from "the Gay Agenda." I almost decided to leave Church after sacrament meeting (after all, I was in Utah—I could walk back to my daughter's home!). But years of commitment to attending Church won out, and I simply sat near the door so I could slip out if the situation became too ugly for me.

When the bishop began the meeting, he spoke with compassion of the hearts that were hurting in the room. He then said that he would read the letter, and there would be no discussion afterwards. As soon as he was done, he would end the meeting and go to his office. If any of us had questions or comments, we could speak with him one-on-one, and he would stay at Church until everyone had a chance to express their thoughts.

Then he tenderly read the letter and left the room. There was no commentary, no harsh condemnation or predictions of evil outcomes. Everyone quietly followed his example and left without comment. I was so grateful for his sensitivity and modeling of kindness to his ward, as he asked them to consider those hurting hearts. It was a beautiful example of comforting those in need of comfort, and teaching members to consider the impact of their words on each other. I felt deep appreciation for him, and that ward became a safe space for me. (If you are familiar with David Butler's books and YouTube series *Don't Miss This*, my story will not surprise you—he was the bishop.)

A few of the women I interviewed talked about experiences of being in Church when a speaker or teacher said things that cut them to the heart. They slipped out of the room to go cry in the foyer or in their car, and women they didn't know followed them and held them as they wept. That Christlike love creates a feeling of belonging and safety which makes it possible to return to Church the following week. When painful comments are made, we can mourn with those that mourn and feel pain.

We could take another step and respond when offensive things are said in class. There are hurting hearts in the room with hidden sorrows, and hearing someone gently correct a harsh or uninformed comment is salve to their wounds. Elder Renlund advises "Brothers and sisters, not throwing stones is the first step in treating others with compassion. The second step is to try to catch stones thrown by others."[10]

When we open our eyes and hearts, we are better able to see how to create safe spaces and relationships. One way is to be sensitive to those in our church community who don't have the expectation of being partnered and having children. Cindy explains she left the gay community and her relationships to return to Church. But it's not easy. She explains "the hardest part is to be in a community/Church/world-in-general, where getting married and having families and a lifelong companion is the focus of life. But my 'persona/being gay' and moral/Church standards are in direct conflict with allowing the type of connection required to have that relationship in my own life. It's like God saying it is not good that the man (or woman) should be alone, but you, Cindy, have to be alone if you want to be accepted by Me because I did not create you [able] to accomplish my ways as I intended."

Charlotte attended a young single adult ward where there was a lot of emphasis at Church on dating. She did want friends, but she didn't feel comfortable with so much pressure to date guys. "I want to talk about Jesus," she says. "COVID Church has been better because it is more focused on Christ. I can focus more on the core gospel."

Raven describes an excruciating time in her life: "Before my affair, I did have a pretty strong testimony. Afterward I felt an immense amount of guilt. It was so hard to be in sacrament meeting. I started crying through sacrament meeting, having breakdowns almost every Sunday. A couple of women saw that something was wrong. I first opened up to one of those friends. Her response was more gentle and loving than I expected. She encouraged me to talk to the bishop, and it was through my associations at church that I was able to confess my sins and find relief." Her friends not only comforted her with their compassion but also responded to her desire to repent and helped her to find spiritual and emotional healing.

We can individually create a welcoming, safe, empathetic space without compromising our doctrine, our political beliefs, or our integrity. Not only can we; we must. We have a covenant obligation to do so.

LEAD WITH LOVE

Bishops have a tremendous impact on the well-being of their LGBTQ congregants. Focusing on best practices rather than horror stories, we can see the powerful force for good that they can be. Today's leaders are supported with an abundance of resources from the church.[11] These resources teach the doctrine of marriage and discourage behavior outside the bounds the Lord has set, but there is a consistent theme of responding with compassion and listening to understand.

Erin's bishop was instrumental in her successful return to Church, though it happened over a period of several years. If she wasn't at Church, he would call to make sure she was okay. Once after Church he asked, "Why aren't you taking the sacrament?" She said she didn't feel worthy. "I think you should take the sacrament," he said. He encouraged her back into covenant even when she felt weighed down by her own self-judgment. If she hadn't had the bishop she did, she believes she would not have been able to come back because it was so hard to get out of her relationship with her girlfriend. She says, "I remember sitting at the top of a canyon in my girlfriend's arms, and thinking, *This is right, this is what God wants*. At some point, I started to get this nagging feeling "No that's not it. That's not what God wants. He doesn't want me in this relationship."" Her bishop's loving, patient support made it possible for her to return to Church in time.

Eliza is dating women and intends to continue attending Church. When she moved into a new ward, she reached out to the Relief Society president to introduce herself and explain her situation, and she asked the president to put her on the ward council list for people who need to be fellowshipped. She met with her stake president, who treated her with great kindness and said, "I want to understand your experience."

Wendy is eager to have that kind of discussion with her priesthood leaders. "I cannot tell you how frustrating it is to say to leadership that I am here and want/need to have conversations about these things. I have been dismissed and mostly ignored," she says. A number of the women I interviewed said they had met with leaders and offered to be a resource, only to be told they were not needed because there are no LGBTQ members in the ward or stake. It's a bit of a Catch-22; leaders won't respond if they don't see a need, but people won't talk about it if they don't feel safe. In addition, there are straight members who have LGBTQ friends or family members, and their faith is challenged when their Church experience reflects insensitivity or unkindness to their loved ones.

Accurate statistics are hard to come by (I never would have been counted), but we are safe in assuming there are people who experience attraction to their own gender or gender dysphoria in every ward, and every priesthood, Relief Society, Sunday School, seminary, and institute classes. Expect they are there, speak with kindness, catch the stone if someone throws one, and you won't go wrong. As we intentionally create safe environments where vulnerable people can be present without judgment, members will feel more comfortable staying in the room.

One way leaders can send a powerful message about acceptance and inclusion is by asking openly LGBTQ members to participate in various ways, like being given a calling, invited to speak in church, or called to teach in various church organizations and quorums. Their visibility reassures other members who are not yet out that they will not be rejected, relegated to second-class membership, or not trusted to hold a calling or teach. Here are other ways to support LGBTQ members:

- Creating support groups for members and their families.
- Not talking in terms of "us" (Church members) and "them" (LGBTQ). We are all "us."

- Being willing to use terms such as "gay" and "lesbian," and use preferred names and pronouns.[12]
- Local leaders acknowledging that there are LGBTQ members and being inclusive of them in talks and lessons.
- When teaching about families, being sensitive to the gay members who desperately want families and are sacrificing that desire to keep their covenants.
- Sharing current church teachings and policies about same-sex attraction so all members are aware of changes in the last fifty years.
- Not discouraging members from talking about being LGBTQ. If they "come out," they are asking to be seen and accepted.
- Making sure there is no bullying behavior among youth or adults.
- Being aware of the increased risk for suicide and depression. Consider training for youth leaders and others to know how to recognize and help people who are suicidal.
- Being aware of resources, like North Star, that can provide additional support and community to LGBTQ members committed to staying in the Church.

As a young adult, McKell knew the Church was true, but something made her really sad. She realized in the MTC that she was attracted to women. At her MTC exit interview she told her branch president, who was very supportive. He taught her two lessons: the first was the difference between sin and weakness. Weakness can strengthen our relationship with God if we use it to bring us closer to Him. He also recommended bringing more light into her life and loving women in a Christlike way.

Her mission president helped her to navigate how to be gay and a member of the Church. The sister training leaders directed her to North Star, and her mission president gave her permission to watch Voices of Hope videos. Her leaders all reinforced the truth that God loved her, and He would still love her.

What better and truer message can families, ward members, and leaders give to LGBTQ members than this? "God loves you, I love you, you don't have to do this alone." As Mae advises, "Just love the heck out of your members and let the policy follow."

Notes for Chapter Sixteen

1   M. Russell Ballard, "Hope in Christ," *Liahona*, May 2021.

2   This is an excellent resource for families. You can access it at https://familyproject.sfsu.edu/family-education-booklet-lds.

3   Dallin H. Oaks, quoted in "Church Updates Resources Addressing Same-Sex Attraction," *Church News*, October 25, 2016, https://www.churchofjesuschrist.org/church/news/church-updates-resources-addressing-same-sex-attraction?lang=eng.

4   Quentin L. Cook, "Let Us Be at the Forefront," video on Church website; available at https://www.churchofjesuschrist.org/topics/gay/videos/let-us-be-at-the-forefront?lang=eng.

5   Marvin J. Ashton, "The Tongue Can Be A Sharp Sword," *Ensign*, May 1992.

6   Dallin H. Oaks, quoted by Sydney Walker, "'The pioneer legacy is a legacy of inclusion,' President Oaks declares," *Church News*, Leaders and Ministry, July 20, 2021, www.thechurchnews.com.

7   John K. Carmack, "When Our Children Go Astray," *Ensign*, Feb 1997.

8   Dieter F. Uchtdorf, "The Merciful Obtain Mercy," *Ensign*, May 2012.

9   "Letter from First Presidency regarding same-sex marriage," *Church News*, Archives, July 9, 2015, www.thechurchnews.com.

10 Dale G. Renlund, "Infuriating Unfairness," *Liahona*, May 2021.

11 These are a few that are readily accessible on the church website:

- https://www.churchofjesuschrist.org/study/manual/counseling-resources/same-sex-attraction?lang=eng

- https://www.churchofjesuschrist.org/topics/gay?lang=eng

- https://www.churchofjesuschrist.org/study/manual/gospel-topics/same-sex-attraction?lang=eng

- https://www.churchofjesuschrist.org/topics/transgender?lang=eng

- https://www.churchofjesuschrist.org/study/manual/general-handbook/38-church-policies-and-guidelines?lang=eng#title_number109

For example, from Counseling Resources: "Some members may feel same-sex attraction or identify as gay, lesbian, or bisexual. As you seek the guidance of the Holy Ghost and take the time to educate yourself about the needs of God's children who experience same-sex attraction or identify as gay, you will develop charity and your capacity to minister will be magnified.

"Feeling same-sex attraction or choosing to use a sexual identity label (such as gay, lesbian, or bisexual) is not a sin and does not violate Church policy. Words like gay and lesbian mean different things to different people. Identifying as gay may mean a member experiences same-sex attraction but chooses not to act on these feelings. This label may also describe how they express themselves emotionally, physically, romantically, sexually, or politically. Do not assume an individual is breaking the law of chastity because they use a sexual identity label."

12 "If a member decides to change his or her preferred name or pronouns of address, the name preference may be noted in the preferred name field on the membership record. The person may be addressed by the preferred name in the ward." "Transgender Individuals" *General Handbook: Serving in The Church of Jesus Christ of Latter-day Saints*, 38.6.23, churchofjesuschrist.org. Accessed electronically August 12, 2021.

Chapter Seventeen

ACCEPTANCE AND EXPERIENCE

During the interviews for this book, I met women who are brave, wise, kind, compassionate, and resilient, as well as tortured, filled with self-doubt, in turmoil, fearful, and confused. Their engagement with the Church ranges from active and complicated to non-existent. They may be in mixed-orientation marriages, celibate, or dating women and planning to marry. They have met me with vulnerability and trust.

I ended every interview with the same question: "What would you say to a woman who is at the beginning of this journey?" They answered with deep emotion in their voices and compassion for that woman, sharing what they felt was their most important message.

Sky: You can be happy, but it isn't easy. Struggles make us stronger and build us up in ways we can't get in our comfort zone. I've learned to look at every trial as opportunity for growth. Instead of "Why me?" I ask "What can I learn from this; what are You trying to teach me? Show me where to go from here. Where would You have me go; what would You have me do; what do I need to learn to become the person You want me to be?" He has already given me what I need to be happy, and I can trust Him. I look around me and see how many people have stepped up and made themselves my family. I'm happier than I've ever been in my life.

Jane: Breathe. It's okay, it's okay. You're not alone. You're not going to have answers anytime soon. Have self-compassion. Think of other times you didn't know how to do something, and it took a while to become good at it. You'll figure out what you want. You've got to have someone you can talk to who won't tell you one way or another. What you want will be really loud at some point. Work at reconciling belief and faith.

Marisol: Heavenly Father loves you. It doesn't matter how you feel or what you have done, Heavenly Father loves you and will love you forever. There are people who will hurt you, but Christ can be healing. I prayed, "What am I supposed to do with all the pieces of my broken heart?" and received the prompting "You just need to love all the broken pieces of your heart. If you allow me, we're going to put the pieces back together." My journey will be so long, but it is worth it. He will be next to me.

Linda: I'd just listen. Every person is different—we all fall on the spectrum; you can't give advice until you know their story. Then I'd tell them to take it slow and the importance of the word AND. We spend a lot of time in opposing feelings. "And" gives you permission to wrestle with two opposing spaces. It's a lot easier for women to hide, to hide in marriages and to hide in the gospel. But our voices need to be there so other women have the example of honoring who they are and finding space to be in church and be authentic.

Jo: It's okay that you feel this way. That attraction and that experience can mean all kinds of things for you. Stay close to the Lord, be open to whatever He would bring you, even if you don't understand. Listen to the spirit; stay close to Him. It's okay to be attracted to women and be a disciple of Christ. You can live with ambiguity. You don't have to know the answer to everything.

AJ: If it's not okay, it's not the end yet. Eventually it will all make sense. It's not going to be now. Being honest with God makes it easier to pray and read scriptures.

Phoebe: You are not alone. There are more of us than you know. You can feel and grieve whatever you've lost. Nothing you feel is wrong. You are entitled to any amount of support you want. If you stay secure in your identity as a child of God, you will know Heavenly Father and Heavenly Mother love you and Heaven is open.

Zeilah: Don't be scared of who you're going to find inside yourself. You are God's and He made you and loves you. Don't be scared of what you're going to find—you won't find anything He doesn't already know and love. He loves you not in spite of being gay, but He loves you because He made you like that.

Daniela: Even before we know how we identify, or what will happen, there's a lot of fear and shame. There are so many voices in our heads and hearts. Connect with Heavenly Father—His love is not going to go anywhere. Labels or people's reactions won't change that. If you're able to feel that love, it will decrease feelings of fear and shame.

Beth: There is great healing and comfort and compassion to be found in the light. When you keep this to yourself, and carry that shame, it eats away at your soul. The gospel of Jesus Christ has beautiful teachings about forgiveness. We are mortals having a mortal experience, and we only have so much control over our feelings. Same-sex attraction is rooted in God-given love. By letting those feelings out and letting them see the light, shame doesn't accumulate. The Spirit has a hard time getting through shame.

Mae: God loves you as you are. You are fully and wholly loved as you are. Whatever journey or path that will make you whole and happy, that will make you feel worth, is what God wants as well. We are here to have joy. Sometimes it changes; at certain points in your life, cleaving to covenants is the right thing, at other times it may look different, but regardless of your choices you are loved. Love is also loving yourself as you are.

Wendy: Above all else, have piles and piles of excessive amounts of grace for yourself. Shame is a product of your upbringing, not of God. It's a tool of the adversary to keep us disconnected from other human beings. We should be connected to each other. Even if God's goal is to get us all to the highest level of the celestial kingdom, he's got a bazillion years to get us there.

Rebecca: Give yourself space to feel what you're going to feel, and don't judge yourself for it. Take things slow and involve God with every decision. A friend said, "Who is the God of your understanding?

What does God think about you? What does your experience say God is like?" God has given me a space to find my own path. My family has given me space to find my own way without shaming or preaching to me.

Charlotte: You aren't alone. There are so many people willing to be with you and walk with you. It will get easier but harder at first. The only way out is through. Find an awesome therapist and your people who will support you, no matter what you do.

Lydia: You don't have to fight with yourself anymore over this; there's a peace that comes with acceptance.

As I listen to these women's voices, I feel the compassion in God's gentle promise: "ye are little children, and ye have not as yet understood how great blessings the Father hath in his own hands and prepared for you; and ye cannot bear all things now; nevertheless, be of good cheer, for I will lead you along" (D&C 78:17-18).

Elder Dale G. Renlund's words offer additional perspective: "If Christ were teaching a child to walk and the child stumbled, He would help the child get up and encourage the next steps. Christ is the helper and consoler. His ways bring joy and hope—eventually and always."[1]

I add my witness to theirs. Jesus has been my helper and consoler. I have shared with you some snapshots of my life, pieces that I hope will inform and reassure you of God's love for LGBTQ women and their place in His kingdom. It's not a complete picture—who really sees that but the Savior? I see my own life only through a glass darkly[2], though as the Lord offers illumination of one piece or another, I gradually increase in understanding and in greater love for His wisdom and creativity and tender mercies. His loving-kindness is constant for us, my dear friends, and I pray that my witness helps you to feel and believe in His love.

Notes for Chapter Seventeen

1 Dale G. Renlund, "Choose You This Day," *Ensign*, November 2018.

2 "For now we see through a glass, darkly; but then face to face: now I know in part; but then shall I know even as I am known." (1 Cor. 13:12)

Appendix

This chart was developed by the Walk Beside Me support group for parents of LGBTQ children. It is useful in identifying the outdated teachings many of us grew up with and replacing them with current instruction (as of September 2021). Much of the discomfort members may feel with LGBTQ people can be traced to these obsolete teachings, which can then be replaced with more light and knowledge.

OBSOLETE TEACHINGS:	CURRENT TEACHINGS:	CHURCH SOURCES:
Being LGBT is a choice.	Being LGBT is not a choice. The church has no position on the causes of being LGBT.	• "Perhaps such susceptibilities are inborn or acquired without personal choice or fault." Elder Oaks, "Same-Gender Attraction," *Ensign*, Oct 1995 • "Even though individuals do not choose to have such [same-sex] attractions, they do choose how to respond to them." Elder Ballard, "The Lord Needs You Now," *Ensign*, Sept 2015 • "We may not know precisely why some people feel attracted to others of the same sex, but for some it is a complex reality and part of the human experience." Church Website: Gospel Topics • "The Church does not take a position on the cause of same-sex attraction." General Handbook: Policies on Moral Issues: 38.6.12
Being LGBT is a sin. Being LGB is at odds with being a member of the church.	Being LGBT is not a sin. Identifying as LGBT is not a sin. Same-sex sexual relations are a sin.	• "Let us be clear: The Church of Jesus Christ of Latter-day Saints believes that 'the experience of same-sex attraction is a complex reality for many people. The attraction itself is not a sin...' Elder Ballard, "The Lord Needs You Now," *Ensign*, Sept 2015 • "While same-sex attraction is not a sin, it can be a challenge. While one may not have chosen to have these feelings, he or she can commit to keep God's commandments." Official Statement on same-sex attraction from the Church website • "Same-gender attraction is not a sin, but acting on those feelings is..." Elder Holland, "Helping those who Struggle with Same-gender Attraction," *Ensign*, Oct 2007
LGB people are broken and need to be fixed or cured, through prayer,	Methods of "fixing" LGB people are not effective and can be damaging.	• "Avoid promising a reduction or elimination of same-sex attraction in

fasting, repentance, conversion therapy, or heterosexual marriage.	A change in attraction should not be expected or demanded.	exchange for faithfulness." Church Website: Same-Sex Attraction • "Family Services has a longstanding and express policy against using therapies that seek to 'repair,' 'convert,' or 'change' sexual orientation, such as from homosexual to heterosexual. Research demonstrates that electric shock, aversion and other analogous therapies are [ineffective] and harmful to youth who experience same-sex attraction." Church Website: Official Statement • "Marriage should not be recommended as a way to eliminate or reduce same-sex attraction." Counseling Resources for Leaders, Same-Sex Attraction • "...a change in attraction should not be expected or demanded as an outcome by parents or leaders." Church Website: Same-Sex Attraction
Acting on LGB feelings is apostasy. Those in same sex marriage are apostates and must be excommunicated.	You can be LGB and be a member in good standing with the church. Acting on LGB feelings is treated the same way as immoral conduct in heterosexual relationships. Same sex marriages no longer mandate a withdrawal of church membership or are defined as apostasy.	• Immoral conduct in heterosexual and homosexual relationships will be treated in the same way. *The Church News* • Same-sex marriage no longer mandates withdrawal of church membership. General Handbook: Church Policies and Guidelines • The church will no longer characterize same-gender marriage by a Church member as apostasy. *The Church News* • If members feel same-sex attraction and are striving to live the law of chastity, leaders support and encourage them in their resolve. These members may receive Church callings, hold temple recommends, and receive temple ordinances if they are worthy. Male members may receive and exercise the priesthood. General Handbook: Church Policies and Guidelines
Transgender people must be excommunicated, and cannot be baptized.	Transgender people may be baptized and may still enjoy full fellowship. Some membership restrictions could apply to transgender members who transition.	• "It is always important to acknowledge the reality of another person's feelings. We shouldn't deny that someone feels a certain way. We take the reality where it is, and we go from there." Church Website: Transgender: Supporting Others

| | All transgender people are welcome to attend Sunday meetings and participate in social events of the church. | • Transgender people may be baptized but are encouraged not to transition. General Handbook: Church Policies and Guidelines
• Transgender people who have completed a medical transition may still be baptized with the First Presidency's approval but will have some membership restrictions. General handbook: 38.2.3.14
• Transgender members using hormone therapy to prevent gender dysphoria or suicidal ideation may still enjoy full fellowship. General Handbook: Church Policies and Guidelines
• People who identify themselves as transgender should be treated with sensitivity, kindness, compassion, and Christlike love. General Handbook: Frequently Asked Questions
• All [transgender people] are welcome to attend sacrament meeting, other Sunday meetings, and social events of the Church. General Handbook: 38.1.1
• Transgender members who transition will experience some membership restrictions, which "include receiving or exercising the priesthood, receiving or using a temple recommend, and receiving some Church callings. Although some privileges of Church membership are restricted, other Church participation is welcomed." Church Website: Transgender |
| Do not use labels homosexual, gay, or lesbian to identify people, don't let members identity that way.

Members should use "same-sex attracted" exclusively instead of other labels.

Transgender members can only have their birth name on the membership record. | It is not a sin for LGBT people to use their own labels, preferred names and pronouns, nor does it violate church policy.

Our prophet has used the terms LGBT, lesbian, gay, bisexual and transgender in talks.

Members can use those words too, and use preferred pronouns and names. | • Feeling same-sex attraction or choosing to use a sexual identity label (such as gay, lesbian, or bisexual) is not a sin and does not violate Church policy. Words like gay and lesbian mean different things to different people. Identifying as gay may mean a member experiences same-sex attraction but chooses not to act on these feelings. This label may also describe how they express themselves emotionally, physically, romantically, sexually, or politically. Church website: Counseling Resources
• President Nelson used the words lesbian, gay, bisexual and transgender as well as the acronym LGBT over the pulpit to address members who identify |

		that way during a 2019 speech at BYU. • "Ward members and leaders may use the preferred pronouns and name for a transgender member, and note those preferences on the membership record." General Handbook: Church Policies and Instructions
Homosexuality is contagious. People who are LGBT are likely pedophiles.	Being LGBT is not contagious. Being LGBT does not increase the risk of pedophilia.	• "Help individuals understand that being around those who experience same-sex attraction does not mean they will also experience same-sex attraction and that the experience of same-sex attraction does not increase the risk of pedophilia." Church website: Counseling Resources
Members who are LGBTQ should not tell anyone besides their priesthood authority. They should not come out publicly. Members who are 'out' are assumed to be sexually active.	Coming out is encouraged by leaders to reduce depression or self-harm. Do not assume a person is breaking the law of chastity because they use a sexual identity label.	• Leaders should "help a member to disclose feelings of same-sex attraction to trusted individuals. Thoughtfully disclosing these feelings is not only helpful but could potentially protect some individuals against depression or self-harm." Church Website: Counseling Resources • "Words like gay and lesbian mean different things to different people. Identifying as gay may mean a member experiences same-sex attraction but chooses not to act on these feelings. This label may also describe how they express themselves emotionally, physically, romantically, sexually, or politically. Do not assume an individual is breaking the law of chastity because they use a sexual identity label." Church Website: Counseling Resources • "If you decide to share your experiences of feeling same-sex attraction or to openly identify as gay, you should be supported and treated with kindness and respect, both at home and in church." Church Website: Same-Sex Attraction: Individuals
Church members must not publicly support gay marriage, LGBTQ people, gay rights, march in a pride parade or belong to LGBT organizations.	The church supports many gay rights (e.g., housing and employment protections) and teaches members to obey, honor, and sustain the law.	• Sis. Marriott, in an official Church news conference: "This [LGBT rights] movement arose after centuries of ridicule, persecution and even violence against homosexuals. Ultimately, most of society recognized that such treatment was simply wrong, and that such basic human rights as securing a

Doing so could mean a loss of a temple recommend or withdrawal of church membership.	The church supported the LoveLoud festival for LGBT youth. Members may support LGBT people, support gay marriage and gay rights, march in a Pride parade to support LGBT people, and belong to LGBT organizations for church members such as Affirmation or Mormons Building Bridges. Members can do those things both privately and publicly or on social media. Members doing these things should not be at risk of losing their membership or temple recommend.	job or a place to live should not depend on a person's sexual orientation." • Pres. Oaks, at the same news conference: "We call on local, state and the federal government to serve all of their people by passing legislation that protects…the rights of our LGBT citizens in such areas as housing, employment and public accommodation in hotels, restaurants and transportation —protections which are not available in many parts of the country." • "We applaud the LoveLoud Festival for LGBT youth's aim to bring people together to address teen safety and to express respect and love for all of God's children. We join our voice with all who come together to foster a community of inclusion in which no one is mistreated because of who they are or what they believe." Church Statement on LoveLoud Festival • In a 2015 interview with KUTV in Salt Lake City, Elder D. Todd Christofferson was asked if members who actively advocated for support for gay marriage would jeopardize their membership. He said members would be in trouble only for "supporting organizations that promote opposition or positions in opposition to the church's." Backing marriage equality on social media sites, including on Facebook or Twitter, "is not an organized effort to attack our effort," Christofferson said in the interview, "or our functioning as a church." The KUTV interviewer asked further if a Latter-day Saint could "hold those beliefs even though they are different from what you teach at the pulpit?" Yes, the apostle answered. • In a *SLT* interview: "'What about LDS who support same-sex marriage privately among family and friends or publicly by posting entries on Facebook, marching in pride parades or belonging to gay-friendly organizations such as Affirmation or Mormons Building Bridges? Can they do so without the threat of losing their church membership or temple privileges?' Christofferson: 'We have individual members in the church with a variety of

		different opinions, beliefs and positions on these issues....In our view, it doesn't really become a problem unless someone is out attacking the church and...its leaders —if that's a deliberate and persistent effort and trying to get others to follow them, trying to draw others away, trying to pull people, if you will, out of the church or away from its teachings and doctrines. That's very different, he said, than someone who backs a group such as Affirmation.'"
Family and church members should exclude or shun LGBT people.	Members should express love and outreach. No family should exclude LGBT members from the family circle. It is unacceptable to reject a gay child.	• President Oaks "strongly condemned parents who would throw a gay child out of their home. 'That is not acceptable behavior.'" *Salt Lake Tribune*, Mar 2015 • Encourage family members to love the family member and accept the individual. Church website: Counseling Resources • Elder Cook: "As a church, nobody should be more loving and compassionate...Let us be at the forefront in terms of expressing love, compassion, and outreach. Let's not have families exclude or be disrespectful of those who choose a different lifestyle as a result of their feelings about their gender." • "No family who has anyone who has a same-gender issue should be excluded from the family circle. They need to be part of the family circle...I feel very strongly about this. It's a very important principle." Church website: Church News article
There is no place for an LGBT member in our church.	All are welcomed in the Lord's Church. Members need to ensure that everyone has a spiritual home where they are loved and can serve the Lord.	• Elder Ballard: "I want anyone who is a member of the Church who is gay or lesbian to know I believe you have a place in the kingdom and I recognize that sometimes it may be difficult for you to see where you fit in the Lord's Church, but you do. We need to listen to and understand what our LGBT brothers and sisters are feeling and experiencing. Certainly we must do better than we have done in the past so that all members feel they have a spiritual home where their brothers and sisters love them and where they have

		a place to worship and serve the Lord." BYU Devotional 2017
In the past, words such as "abomination" were used to describe LGBT people. Those words have been replaced by teachings that promote love, compassion, and empathy.	Everyone on earth is a beloved child of God and our fellow sibling in Christ and deserve to be treated with respect and dignity.	• Pres. Nelson, 2021: "We are brothers and sisters, each of us the child of a loving Father in Heaven… It behooves each of us to do whatever we can in our spheres of influence to preserve the dignity and respect every son and daughter of God deserves. We need to foster a fundamental respect for the human dignity of every human soul, regardless of their color, creed, or cause. And we need to work tirelessly to build bridges of understanding…I plead with us to work together for peace, for mutual respect, and for an outpouring of love for all of God's children." "During the Savior's earthly mission, He constantly ministered to those who were excluded, marginalized, judged, overlooked, abused, and discounted. As His followers, can we do anything less?The answer is no!" • Pres. Nelson: "If we have any hope of reclaiming the goodwill and sense of humanity for which we yearn, it must begin with each of us, one person at a time…Expand our circle of love to embrace the whole human family." *Liahona*, Sept 2021 article • Pres. Nelson: "[W]e care deeply about every child of God, regardless of age, personal circumstances, gender, sexual orientation, or other unique challenges." BYU Dev. Sept 2019 • "The Church calls on all people to abandon attitudes and actions of prejudice toward any group or individual… They strive to be persons of goodwill toward all, rejecting prejudice of any kind. This includes prejudice based on race, ethnicity, nationality, tribe, gender, age, disability, socioeconomic status, religious belief or nonbelief, and sexual orientation." General Handbook: 38.6.14

About the Author

Meghan Decker is a respected writer, speaker, and gay Latter-day Saint. She is coauthor of *Reaching for Hope: An LDS Perspective on Recovering from Depression*, which has provided insight for thousands of readers who experience depression. Her new book, *Tender Leaves of Hope: Finding Belonging as LGBTQ Latter-day Saint Women*, shares her own experience and amplifies the voices of scores of LGBTQ women who are seeking to hear God in their lives. Meghan has published in *LDS Living, Meridian Magazine,* and *The Friend*. She and her husband, David, have five daughters and fifteen grandchildren, and they enjoy gathering to explore, eat, and trade book recommendations.

Notes

Notes

Notes

Notes

Notes

You've dreamed of accomplishing your publishing goal for ages—holding *that* book in your hands. We want to partner with you in bringing this dream to light.

Whether you're an aspiring author looking to publish your first book or a seasoned author who's been published before, we want to hear from you. Please submit your manuscript to

CEDARFORT.SUBMITTABLE.COM/SUBMIT

CEDAR FORT PUBLISHES BOOKS
IN THE FOLLOWING GENRES

- LDS Nonfiction
- General Nonfiction
- Juvenile & YA
- Cookbooks
- Biographies
- Children's Books
- Self-Help
- Comic & Activity books
- Children's books with customizable character illustrations